KEEP IT SIMPLE

Also by Terry Bradshaw with David Fisher

It's Only a Game

KEEP IT SIMPLE

TERRY BRADSHAW
WITH
DAVID FISHER

ATRIA BOOKS
New York   London   Toronto   Sydney   Singapore

ATRIA BOOKS
1230 Avenue of the Americas
New York, NY 10020

ISBN: 0-7434-1730-5

First Atria Books hardcover printing October 2002

10   9   8   7   6   5   4   3   2   1

ATRIA BOOKS is a trademark of Simon & Schuster, Inc.

For information regarding special discounts for bulk purchases,
please contact Simon & Schuster Special Sales at 1-800-456-6798
or business@simonandschuster.com

Printed in the U.S.A.

DEDICATION

My previous book, *It's Only a Game,* was dedicated to my brothers, with the understanding that they would not be sharing in the proceeds. A dedication, I explained, is worth more than money. It expresses deep feelings of love and appreciation that no amount of money can buy.

While I'm not real sure they accepted that reasoning, they definitely continued to love me as their brother and their friend.

I would like to dedicate this book to two men who have changed my life, my family therapist, Bill Bush, and the pastor of my church, Dr. Nathan Tucker.

Number one is Bill Bush. How in the world can I possibly put a therapist before a preacher? But the fact is that before I got to the preacher I had to get some help, and this is the man who helped me understand who I am and why I made the choices that I have made. It was through Bill Bush that I began to accept responsibility for making those choices.

While doing so makes it much more difficult to blame former coaches or ex-wives for the problems in my life, it is a pretty necessary thing to do in order to regain control. When I met Bill I was in a tailspin, and he basically turned my life around.

He was the man who led me to Dr. Tucker. In addition to the counseling, I needed spiritual help. Bill helped me with my mind, Dr. Tucker helped me focus my heart. After a session with Bill, in which I was forced to come face-to-face with my own face, I'd be so upset, I needed the guidance of Dr. Tucker to move forward.

So Dr. Nathan Tucker, pastor of the Mt. Gilhead Baptist Church, is also number one. In order for me to forgive myself for things that I have done, I needed to know that the Lord forgave me. I had a hard time with that, a hard time. I needed help, and that's what Dr. Tucker provided for me. His wisdom has made my spiritual growth possible.

This book would not have been possible without these two men. I was a different person before they came into my lives. These men were not the slightest bit interested in my celebrity status, my athletic accomplishments, my glib manner. They cared only about me as a human being struggling through this world. So for their kindness, understanding, and love, I am pleased to dedicate this book to them. I love them both.

Terry Bradshaw

P.S. But once again, I want both of these gentlemen to know they ain't sharing in the proceeds.

TABLE OF CONTENTS

CHAPTER I

An Important Chapter in My Life

WELCOME TO MY BOOK, LADIES AND GENTLEMEN, AND thank you very much for coming to this page today. Let me ask you this question: How many of you reading here have heard my album of gospel songs? Now don't you be shy, speak right up, right out loud. Anybody looks at you funny, you just tell them you're talking to a book. I promise you, they won't bother you again.

Just be grateful that all I asked you to do was say a few words out loud. Usually when I address people I begin by asking them to smile. I love to see people smiling. Love it. A smile is the mirror to the soul. It's a reflection of the character that's inside you. It reflects exactly how you feel about yourself. It tells the world, I'm happy! So go ahead and smile. I mean, you paid for all that dental work, you might just as well show it. When you buy a big expensive car you don't keep it locked in the garage. With all the money you've spent at the dentists don't keep those teeth locked in your mouth! That's right, show off that big Buick grill of a mouth!

And then I usually ask people to turn to the side and look

at the person right next to them directly in the eyes. And shake their hand. Get to know them. Then after you get to know them, if they're nice enough give them a hug. Just go ahead and hug on 'em. And then I ask them to kiss—wait, don't you go doing that. You'd definitely have a tough time convincing a judge that you kissed a stranger because a book told you to.

Obviously there is a big difference between reading a book and listening to me speak in person, but some things are exactly the same. Let me tell you, when I ask an audience how many people have heard my gospel album those people usually give me exactly the same answer I get when I ask that question to people reading my book; total silence. My friends, if you really want to hear my album you just go on into your local record store and look for it; though you might want to look in the section labeled "landfill." When an album is successful it goes "gold," my album went "lead." That didn't bother me, I knew I wasn't really a singer. What I was, was the quarterback of the Super Bowl champions. That's a well-known rule; you win a Super Bowl you get to record an album.

Not really a singer is only one of the many things I am not. Besides married, I mean. I am definitely not married. I am also not a movie actor, a television show host, or a talk-radio host, although I've also tried to do those things. Unsuccessfully. And those aren't the only things I've failed at, those are just some of the highlights. I've failed at a great variety of jobs. If there is one subject at which I am very good, it's failure. If failing was considered a profession, I'd be a legend at it.

But I got to record several albums, host my own TV show, appear in movies, host a talk-radio show, and make numerous commercials because I was very good at handing off a football to another man or passing it to a receiver and letting him run with it. Let him get hit by the big guys. That was my primary experience, handing off a football or passing it. So when record producers heard my voice they probably said, "Maybe he don't sound that great, but he won a Super Bowl." Or when television producers saw me acting they might have decided, "That boy sure doesn't look that good, but he won a Super Bowl!"

Can I have an amen on winning the Super Bowl, please?

You win just one Super Bowl and people'll amen you to death.

Lemme have an amen on amening! Hallelujah to that, Brother Terry!

There was one other thing I could do. I could talk. I mean, I could definitely talk. I could fill a silence better than jelly filled a doughnut, better than a cow filled a milk pitcher, better than Pamela Anderson filled—well, you get the concept. So I began making speeches. I spoke anyplace they would have me. I spoke in auditoriums, I spoke in gymnasiums, I spoke standing up in the back of a '52 pick-up truck. And I became very successful. In fact, by the time I realized I had nothing of true importance to say it was too late, I was already a big success at making speeches.

One reason I have been successful at it is because I begin almost every speech by making a promise that I know I can fulfill. And I hereby make that same promise to you right on this very page: By the time you finish this book you will feel better about yourself. Because after you read my words you will know for certain that you are more intelligent than at least one person in the world.

Here's a little hint; most times when somebody tells you they are not very smart they are trying to outsmart you: "Ah, shucks, ya'all, I'm too dang dumb to know that this here marshmallow roaster is worth a lot more than the $99 in three easy installments I'm selling it to you for."

I am not trying to outsmart you. Not me. Not with my family background. When I got my job at the Fox network, for example, my Momma was just thrilled. "Baby, that's wonderful," she said. When I asked her why, she told me, "'Cause it's much easier to spell than ESPN."

Throughout my entire professional football career I was known for being dumb. That was my professional image. Dick Butkus was ferocious. Walter Payton was as elusive as mercury. Terry Bradshaw was dumb. D-u-m. Dumb. Bradshaw was so dumb he couldn't pass a physical. In the off-season Bradshaw works as a test dummy. And truthfully it hurt me when people said that. It was said about me that I couldn't spell "cat" even if they spotted me the *c* and the *t*. Other people laughed. But it was not something I thought was funny or clever. It was not an image I embraced. I wasn't even smart enough to realize how beneficial that image might be to me later in my life. Being dumb became my character.

You ever see me doing a commercial? I'm the one fishing in the swimming pool. I'm the one driving two ways on a one-way street. I'm the one getting insulted by a puppet.

It is a character that has worked very well for me. For example, when I make speeches to large groups—not like right now when I'm addressing you personally—I explain that I'm not really as dumb as my image. I have a PE degree from Louisiana Tech, I say proudly. I have a PE degree! Some people laugh when I say that, but there's nothing at all funny about a PE degree. When I earned that degree my family was mighty proud of me. Not counting my older brother, I was the very first person in our family to graduate from college. Although admittedly my grandfather, my pawpaw, didn't quite understand my degree. "A Pee degree?" he kept asking. "Heck, when I was coming up they didn't have to teach it, they just sent you out back behind the house and told you not to do it upwind."

Truth is, though, all along I was smart enough to understand that I wasn't really that smart. That was an important piece of information. At times I've struggled with life the way an ant struggles with a suitcase. I have a perfect record in marriage, for example: three marriages, three divorces, a perfect record. I've made and lost and made and lost a considerable amount of money. I've done so many things in my life that even I don't understand—buying two ostrich eggs for $7,000 would be a particularly fine example of that—that I no longer worry about it.

But for a long time I did want to understand my life. Part of my problems, I discovered as an adult, came from the fact that I had ADD, attention deficit disorder. That made it hard for me to focus on things I didn't really like. School, for instance. It also made it difficult for me to retain information. I'd read a question on a test, I'd know the answer, but before I could write it down I'd not only forget the answer, I'd forget the question. I didn't do well on tests. The problem with that is when you're young and people tell you that you're not very smart you tend to believe them. No matter what happens later in life that leaves pretty big scars on your personality. No question that it shaped me. I found that in the classroom I couldn't compete academically—but I could definitely make people laugh. I would say funny things, most of the time intentionally. So I grew up just loving the sound of laughter. And I could compete with anyone on the football field. I could throw a football farther than anyone else. So I grew up throwing a football and making people laugh. Not at the same time, of course.

It made growing up interesting. It also made being grown-up difficult. So much so that I've spent considerable time in therapy. In my life I've been to see five different therapists. The first time I went to a therapist I was so embarrassed about being there that I made up problems to impress him. I went to him once. The second counselor I went to was much too direct for me. "Look, Terry," he told me, "you're with the wrong gal. There's nothing wrong with her, she's just the wrong girl for you." That was a pretty shocking thing to hear. Maybe if he had just sort of eased into it—"You know, Terry, the crops need to be picked and she doesn't know how to drive a tractor" or "You know, Terry, when you're climbing a mountain it's better to take a mule than a duck"—I might have figured it out. I could have accepted it, but he just told me right off. So it was difficult for me to accept; some things in life are just cut and dried when we need them to be folded and wet. If he had told me I was driving the wrong car maybe I would have traded it in. But I couldn't do that with my wife. You can't just take her to a Used Wife Lot and trade her on in for a new model. That'd be some good business, but you can't do it. So instead I changed therapists.

Then I went to see two different women therapists. Both of them were very nice, but I was just uncomfortable telling my problems to women. It was amazing. I needed help, and either of these women was more than qualified to help me, but my biggest problem at that time was with a woman so I was embarrassed to be telling a woman about it. I didn't want so much to impress them, as I did the male therapist, as entertain them. I'm always most comfortable with women when I can get them laughing. So I'd be telling them my best stories about my mother's tooth or going to a restaurant and ordering steak tartar medium well.

But the first woman therapist confused me so much I had to go to the second woman therapist just to interpret what the first one was telling me: Oh, that's what she meant. Wow, that's pretty smart. Then I'd run right back to the first one with my response.

It wasn't working. My friends, I flunked therapy. Just downright dunked it. And then I met Mr. Bill Bush. Now admittedly Bill Bush has a weight problem. I don't know if it's because he got weaned off the breast too young, which I think might be a common problem among therapists; and he does tend to cry pretty easily, which he tells me is because he is in touch with his feelings; and he definitely stutters when he is asking me about any sexual problems, which naturally I don't have any of—no how no way do I have any sexual problems thank you very much.

But he has a nice soft voice. And he has a way of getting right to the core of the situation: "Terry, I don't think it has anything to do with her deep-rooted feelings of hostility toward men based on her own early insecurity, I think she just wasn't interested in going to the Monster Truck Rally." And also, he is a Christian counselor, meaning that in addition to using the accepted techniques of traditional therapy, he often uses basic scriptural principles that apply not only to my specific problems, but also to basic daily life skills. And most of all he helped me change my life. He helped me to understand the difference between those things I could not change and those things that I could change and to accept those things I could not change and fire those people who needed to be fired.

He made me the person that I am today.

That last sentence is what is known in comedic circles as a straight line. You can fill in the punch line to suit your taste. But the fact is, Bill exposed me to some pretty basic truths about my life that I intend to communicate to you. And we're very fortunate to have Bill with us in this chapter, to help you understand me just a little better. This way you won't make the same mistakes I've made, which is definitely the purpose of any self-help motivational-inspirational book.

So without further distraction, my therapist Bill Bush is now going to do his diagnosis of me for you. . . .

"The day Terry arrived at my office for the first time I watched through the window as he got out of his car and looked around. Then he unbuttoned his jeans and tucked his shirttail into his pants. At least he was going to be properly dressed for this meeting with a counselor. I greeted him at the door. He is taller than me but I had more hair, but not too much more. He was all smiles until we began the session and then another Terry appeared. This wasn't the smiling character I had seen on television; this was a man who was strong yet fearful, a man with feet of clay.

"Terry was in the process of separating from his third wife. He wanted to put the relationship back together, but she had different ideas. We talked often during those difficult times. Terry was a broken man and handled his pain with many emotions; he would be alternately angry and deeply sad. It was during this period that he won an Emmy for his work on the Fox NFL Sunday show. 'I do my best work when I'm hurting,' he told me.

"Some of Terry's failings were of his own making. Others just happened. He is a complex man; he is incredibly private, but is exhilarated by people. He wants everyone to like him, a people pleaser, sometimes to his own detriment. He often gives things away in an attempt to please other people; he gave away his shotgun, he gave his former brother-in-law his boat and a brand new truck, he was even about to invest in a former in-law's wooden rocking-horse business.

"While on the surface he appears to be very tough, very strong, a man's man, in fact he is actually a very tender, sensitive person. At one point, for example, we were talking about some of the things he had done in the past, nothing so terrible it couldn't be forgiven, but I pointed out to him, 'Terry, that behavior was wrong.'

"He said, 'I know it was.'

"'Well then,' I said, 'you must feel awfully guilty about it.'

"At that point he just broke into tears, 'I'm just consumed with guilt,' he told me.

"When people say negative things about him he usually acts as if he doesn't care, but it can be very hurtful to him. That is a primary reason he tends to shy away from people and places where he has experienced that emotional pain. That's probably one of the reasons he hasn't spent much time in Pittsburgh since he retired.

"His normal behavioral patterns were certainly impacted negatively by his attention deficit issues, which sometimes caused him to act impulsively. As a student he could not possibly have tested well because he just couldn't remain focused on the questions. He likes to get things done. Even with me he became extremely impatient to finish our counseling sessions. At one point he said to me, 'Why aren't I well yet? I mean, I've paid you all this money and I'm not well yet.'

"To which I responded, 'Terry, I'm not sure you have enough money for that.'

"Terry set out to learn about himself and I think, to a large extent, he has succeeded. At least now he understands why he behaves as he does. And he understands why he so much enjoys the sound of other people laughing . . . "

Thank you very much, Bill, thank you. The check's in the mail. The point that Bill was trying to make is that my life is so messed up how can I give advice that has any value to anyone else? That's a warning from my very own personal therapist. The fact is that I can't help you find the solution to your problems, and please don't expect me to provide the answers. What can I possibly offer you that you don't know? Basically, about all I can do is try to make you feel a little better than you did when you started reading this sentence. Make you smile, and maybe even laugh. I'm being honest. I just flat cannot help you with the serious problems of your life. That's not my job. I'm a mess myself and I brought my therapist here to prove it.

But I'm a wonderful mess. At least that's what my momma tells me. "Oh, Terry, that's okay," she tells me, "you didn't mean to cause that entire company to go out of business. It was their fault; who in the world ever told them to hire you?"

Not me. Definitely not me. If you believe that self-help books or motivational speakers can really help improve your life there is no shortage of them available to take your money. You can read about the *Leadership Secrets of Attila the Hun,* for example, which basically comes down to beating the competition by cutting off their heads and putting them on stakes. Then there is the woman's version of that, *Leadership Secrets of Elizabeth I,* which includes particularly good advice for women who want to defeat Spain. There are books that reveal the secrets of happiness from Shakespeare, Benjamin Franklin, even Robert E. Lee—people who have one thing in common: They're all dead! My question is if they really had these secrets how did the people who wrote these books find out about them in the first place?

One of these people wrote a best-selling book that promises a "ten-minute test that can make your favorite daydream come true." Now I seriously doubt that, because that particular daydream's husband would most definitely have an opinion about this. What am I going to do? Tell him, sorry, but it says right here in this book that my daydream is coming true.

The only people these self-help inspirational books really help are the people who got paid to write them. I promise you, I am not going to make you smarter, younger, or a better leader. You are definitely not going to learn management techniques from me. You aren't going to double your income working from your own home. When I speak to people I tell them right at the beginning not to bother taking any notes, because nothing I am going to say is worthy of writing down. I learned very early it isn't what I said, but how I said it, as long as I said it funny.

It made me proud to hear people saying as they walked out after listening to me speak, "I don't know what he said, but, boy, he was funny saying it." Or, "Boy, that was some speech; it sure used up a lot of words."

I love speaking to people and the only claim I'll make is that they will smile. At least most of the time. One time I was invited to speak at the convention of the National Physicists Society in Washington, D.C. I am not making this up. When I tell you about giant pig eggs I'm pretty definitively making it up, but this story is true. Initially when they asked me to speak I turned them down. I felt this was a group that might not understand my sense of humor. I just didn't believe people who spent their time figuring out the basic structure of the universe would understand the status my grandfather derived in Hall Summit, Louisiana, from having a two-holer in his backyard.

But when this group insisted they wanted me to speak, I agreed. The members had come to Washington from all over the world. They were very wealthy, very successful, they were true intellectuals; these were the kind of people who drink their wine from glasses! For many of them English was a second language, and those people definitely did not speak drawl.

The chairman gave me a rousing introduction, and I was greeted with polite, cordial, lukewarm applause. Maybe some people would have been a little hesitant after that response, but not me, no siree, not me. I took that response as a challenge. I became determined that I was going to reach them with Terry's own brand of homespun humor, I was going to make contact with their emotions, I was going to move them. Move them! I said. Uplift them! Can you hear me, my friends, I was going to give them my A-number-one speech, the big one, the wowser, the neutron bomb of speeches. I don't do it too often, it takes too much out of me to climb to that peak, but these people were going to get it all.

I started that speech and let me tell you something, ladies and gentlemen, if you get to page 150 of this book you will never read about another speech like this one. Oh, my Lord, it was something beautiful to hear. I put everything possible into it. Now generally I sweat easy; I've been known to work up a sweat toweling off after a shower, but this time within minutes I was wringing wet. I got down on the ground, I ripped out my heart and held it up high for them to see. I screamed and I hollered and I whispered, I beseeched these people. I was imploring them. I was a blur on that stage. I knocked over the podium. I was up and down and around. My words were stirring and meaningful and . . . and as I ended this speech I brought myself to tears as I stood there expressing my love for my sweet, beautiful, innocent little girls. When I finished I was dripping wet, totally exhausted.

And I received polite, cordial, lukewarm applause.

I ended up with a migraine headache. Backstage one of the organizers was ecstatic. "That was incredible," she said, "absolutely unbelievable, the best we've ever heard." She asked me if I had any questions.

"Just one," I said. "You got any Demerol?" The best ever? If I was the best, I couldn't begin to imagine the speakers they'd had in previous years. Rainman? Snoop Doggy Dog? Andrew Dice Clay? Marcel Marceau?

I've spoken before literally hundreds of different groups. I've spoken to corporate groups, civic groups; the smallest group I ever spoke in front of was twenty-three people, the top salesmen of a company; the largest group was about ten thousand Amway salespeople. I've spoken in front of ethnic groups, among them the Dallas/Fort Worth Jewish Society. Jewish Texans, who knew? Yippee oi vey! I loved that speech; the people who were introducing me were telling all these "two Jews walked into a bar . . ." jokes and I was writing them down as fast as they told them. When I stood up I noticed that many people in the audience were wearing their skullcaps, their yarmulkes. I'd come a long way—a few years earlier I hadn't even known what a yarmulke was; I'd guessed it was an Israeli car, the Jewish Honda. This time I complimented them, I told them I loved their "Jewish cowboy hats." I've never spoken in front of a predominately African-American group, but I'm ready; I'm waiting on the NAACP to invite me, Brother Terry, yo bro, let's give it up for the cracker from Louisiana.

I speak directly from my heart. I don't plan my speeches, I certainly don't write them down and memorize them. I have a vague concept of where I'm going and how I'm going to get there. There are certain stories I've used many times to make a point. For example, I used to always include some football material. I'd talk about a player we had on the Steelers who wasn't very big of stature, but he was large of heart. What he lacked in size he made up in determination. He succeeded because he believed in himself. In his heart he was a giant. A giant, my friends, a giant. At the training table one day, I remember, they were serving steaks and asking everybody how they wanted them cooked. One by one we gave our orders until the waiter asked him how he wanted his cooked. And this boy said confidently, "Don't worry about me. Just break the horns off of that steer and run him through; I'll just rip me off a piece."

I used to tell stories just like that one but then word got back to me that some of my former teammates didn't quite understand that these stories were complimentary. Not complimentary? In my entire long life—which I intend to be a lot longer—I have never said one single uncomplimentary word about any man weighing more than 275 pounds who can clean and jerk more than his bodyweight. Therefore I dropped most references to my teammates.

I have an admission to make: Some of the facts that you will read in this book aren't the real actual truth. For example, my momma doesn't drive a tractor and have one tooth. That's a character I made up. The actual truth is that Ole Gummy, as we lovingly call her, hasn't driven that tractor since the night she got that welding job. And she's real bright too, follows those directions real well; I remember I walked into the kitchen one day and found her just sitting there staring at a can of frozen orange juice. "Momma," I said, "what are you doing?"

"Well, Baby," she said, "it says right here on the can 'concentrate.' So I am."

Some of the material I use has been distilled from other books that I've read. Read? Did that boy say, read? I read a lot. When I get interested in a subject I become a voracious reader. At my ranch my bookshelves are filled and I've read pretty much every one of those books. I love world history, I'm fascinated by World War II. I've read all of Churchill's books and much of what has been written about Hitler and Stalin. I also read inspirational books and some self-help books. I've read a considerable amount of psychology. I love those basic psychology books, books that make a complicated subject relatively easy to understand, even for me. You know: Run, Jane run. See Jane run—right to the pharmacy for her Prozac.

The books give me a direction; I get a lot of reassurance from them: When I'm done reading them I'm confident that I don't know just as much as these people don't know. As you'll learn, I never, ever quote anyone. I learned that from Mark Twain, I believe, who said, "A man who relies on quoting others is weak of mind!" Or maybe it was Tommy Smothers. The real problem with quotes is that you have to remember them. And sometimes it's difficult to work the few quotes I do know by heart into a speech. For example, growing up I loved The Three Stooges. People don't take them very seriously in the United States, but in France, *Les Trois Stooges*, as they're known, are considered avant-garde comedic geniuses whose work explored the deeper meaning of banging people over the head with rolling pins. I saw every movie they ever made and I definitely could quote them in my speeches, but I haven't been able to figure out how to work "Nyuck, nyuck" into a speech. I can't even figure out how to get it into this book.

I also try to provide for people just a little more information than they originally had. I want you to close this book today knowing more than you did when you opened it. That's important to me. So I'll tell you some of the things I've learned from experience, things I know about from my own life that can be applied to your life. The best way to buy a watermelon, for example. Now men don't know a blessed thing about buying a watermelon. You see men in the supermarket trying to figure out if a watermelon is ripe and what are they doing? They're thumping on it. Am I right? Don't answer, I know I'm right. Men just thump, thump, thump, just like little Peter

Cottontails, thump, thump, thump. And they never, ever buy the first watermelon they thump. Do you know why? Because they know they are not supposed to, that's why. These are educated watermelon thumpers. They never buy the first one they thump because they know somebody is watching them. And probably trying to steal their thumping technique and get the best watermelon. So they have to thump two or three. By that time the other man is thumping his own melons. There is no actual reason to buy the fourth one, but generally that's what men do. Men don't even know what they're listening for, but modern watermelon thumping brings us back to our ancestors who had to grow their own watermelons. When people thump now they listen for a deep sound. A thummmm-mmmmp. That deep sound means there is water in that watermelon and that water is curing the sugar in it. That's going to taste sweet. The key to good thumping is that as soon as you hear a deep, resonant thump, buy that watermelon.

You now know more than you did just three paragraphs ago. I try to educate my audience. One of the things I definitely try to teach is the importance of being able to laugh at yourself. I have found that if people don't like to laugh at themselves there is generally someone nearby willing to do it for them. Is there anything as humorous as someone who takes himself too seriously? Like those people who use cell phones in public and speak loudly enough for everyone around them to hear their entire secret conversation. Love those people: Sell ten thousand shares, pick up the Rolls, make the reservations to Paris. Gotta go now, I'm using up all my free minutes.

Those are the kind of people who need to show their importance. To me, they are just insecure. Sometimes you see them walking down the street looking like they are talking to themselves until you see that they're wearing a headphone. That never impresses me. I grew up watching my momma walking down the street talking away just like them—and that was years before the cell phone was invented.

Truly, I don't understand these people. Never have, never will. Do they really believe that they are so important they can't be away from a phone for a few minutes? What do they think is going to happen: "Oh no! I was away from the phone for three minutes and my wife ran away with the plumber, sold the house, and moved to Des Moines." These are the same people who immediately buy a new phone as soon as a smaller system comes out. For some reason the smaller things get, the more expensive they become. So these people have got to have the smallest cell phone possible just to show other people that they can afford to pay more for less. I had a cell phone once, it was one of the "smart phones." I took it out back and killed it with a shotgun. Didn't seem so smart to me, never said a single word.

Not only do they have cell phones, now they carry Palm Pilots with them. You have to go to class at night, which keeps you away from your family, to learn how to use that Palm Pilot. You have to learn how to take a little stick and punch it to bring up information. Give me a stick and I'll beat the information out of it.

We do need to laugh at ourselves because we are not perfect. Of course for me it's a little easier than for most people; admittedly I've got a lot to work with. When I was young I didn't enjoy it when other people made fun of me, so I decided I would beat them to it. It took me some time to get comfortable making fun of myself, but now I find I'm driving the bandwagon. Maybe a lot of people jump on, but it's always going in the direction of my choice.

The other thing I try not to do is use the same old clichés. I'm not someone who closes the barn door after the chickens have come home to roost. I don't need to tell people things they already know, just so they think I'm smart enough to agree with them. I don't need to tell people things that are obvious: Don't make bad investments. Don't pay any attention to astrologers unless they predict good things. Don't get married and divorced three times. What I do try to do is discuss things that relate directly to real life. My friends, real life can be tough. I mean, tough! It can be real difficult. There are people who look real serious and advise you that when life gives you lemons, make lemonade. That may sound clever but it is just wrong; when was the last time that anybody gave you a lemon? Oh, thank you for this beautiful lemon; it was just what I was hoping to get for my birthday. A much more accurate philosophy—at least applicable to my life—would be: When people throw lemons at you, you just be darn grateful they're not grapefruits!

I want for you the same things you want for me! Or, the same things I hope you want for me—there are probably some Dallas Cowboy fans reading this who are still angry. I want you to be filled with joy inside. I want you happy. I want you to walk around with your head up high. Don't be ashamed of how God made you—you are special. Special! Trust me, you are special. I want you to be so elated by who you are that you just hold your head up high. I want you to find the passion in your life and the freedom to pursue it. I want you to identify those things in your life that are making you unhappy and do something about them. Get rid of them. Annihilate them. Don't just read a book, do something about them.

If you can do all those things, then we are definitely on the same page. This one.

CHAPTER 2

MY BASIC PHILOSOPHY FOR BEATING LIFE'S CHALLENGES

I HAVE BEEN GREATLY BLESSED IN MY LIFE. I KNOW IT and believe me I am very thankful about that. I lived out my dream of playing professional football, I've been paid to act and sing and talk silly, and I have received a lot of awards and honors. In 2001, for example, I was honored with my very own star on the famed Hollywood Walk of Fame. When they first told me I had been selected to be immortalized on the sidewalk, I was a little embarrassed about it. Just exactly what had I done in the entertainment industry to be included among such big stars as Tom Hanks, Rin Tin Tin, Gary Cooper, Lassie, John Wayne, Big Bird, and Liberace? It definitely was not because of my recording career—*Saturday Night Live* had claimed that the very worst album ever recorded; the worst album of all time was *Terry Bradshaw's Calypso Christmas*. But sometimes nice things happen to each of us that we don't really think we deserve, things I call the bonuses of life. This was definitely a bonus of life.

Whatever the reason, I kind of liked it. Just about every major star in entertainment history is represented on that sidewalk. Some people who were successful in more than one field of entertainment had several stars. Gene Autry, for example, was a five-star celebrity. I just had my one little star, for talking on television, but it was still very exciting to me. I brought my family and several of my friends out to Hollywood Boulevard for the dedication. It was pretty cool, there was my name on a bronze plaque embedded in a square right in the middle of the sidewalk. I really was honored. I knew that eventually a lot of people would be looking up to m—well, actually looking down on me.

My daughter Rachel was most excited about the fact that my star was directly next to Paul Newman's. Meaning anybody who wants to get a real good look at Paul Newman's star will just naturally have to stand on me!

The day after the dedication I pulled a cap down over my head and took my daughters shopping at the mall in Century City. Generally there are always a few people who recognize me when I'm out in public, but that day it seemed like every person I passed knew me. I even tried to hide by pulling down my cap a little lower, but as we walked along it seemed like everybody said, Hi, Terry, How you doing, Terry, Congratulations, Terry. Inside, I was feeling proud of the fact that my daughter could see how famous I was; that the old man wasn't just the guy who pays the bills. "Isn't it amazing," I finally said as nonchalantly as I could manage, "I got this hat on and all these people still recognize me. My oh my, how do they know it's me?"

With that, Rachel reached up, took off my cap, and showed it to me. "Dad," she said, frowning, "you got your name right on the front of your hat."

Truth is that after more than three decades of getting my picture in the newspapers I've gotten used to being recognized in public. Everybody knows me, I'm . . . what's his name, you know, that bald guy who speaks real fast on the . . . oh, you know, that football show on Fox on Sundays. Thank you very much, that definitely is me. I remember the very first time someone recognized me; it was just after the Pittsburgh Steelers had drafted me and I'd flown to the city for a press conference. My picture was all over the Pittsburgh newspapers. In Pittsburgh people take their football seriously: I was the *first* coming. As I walked through the airport a man approached me, smiled, and asked, "Aren't you Terry Bradshaw?"

Whew, tough question. I definitely knew I was Terry Bradshaw, I just didn't realize strangers knew it too. For only a split second I wondered if there just might be another Terry Bradshaw out there, the Terry Bradshaw this man wanted to speak with. Congratulations, he said. For what, I wondered, being Terry Bradshaw?

I never have been really comfortable with fame. Basically, I am a shy person. I am. Really. If I think people recognize me or are staring at me I tend to start sweating. It's embarrassing. Now, I know that being famous definitely has certain advantages; in some places I can cash a check with only one form of picture identification. And sometimes nice people offer me a little something extra; like, "You want some extra onions on that hot dog, Mr. Bradshaw?"

In exchange for that I've given up a lot of privacy. I understand people asking for my autograph or asking me to pose with them for a picture; I try to be nice to them, as Bill Bush explained, I try to please people. But what I don't like about it

23

is that many people believe that because I'm on TV I'm special. That I'm different from them. That my life is different from everyone else's.

That just isn't true in my life. I try to lead a very simple life—just like I told Jay Leno last time I was on his show.

The fact is that life is most like a roller coaster—it has its ups and downs. The main difference between the two being that on a roller coaster you pay at the beginning and are supposed to shout "Yippee" on the way down. Being a celebrity, being well known, doesn't insulate me from adversity and pain. What it did was teach me how to hide it better: How you feeling, Ter? Great, thank you for asking—although what I should have said was, "Great, except for the fact that my heart just got ripped right out of my chest and fed to the hogs, I haven't slept in nine weeks, and I just got a postcard from my accountant with a picture of his new house in South America."

Can I have your autograph?

Bad things happen to me just like they happen to everybody else. And I've had to learn how to deal with them. When I went to Ireland with my close friends to play golf at St. Andrews, maybe the most famous golf course in the entire world, we were three minutes late for our tee time. Actually we were three hours early but got caught up in the souvenir shop and missed our tee time, so we were forced to carry our own golf bags the entire round! And people think celebrities don't have to deal with adversity.

Oh, and there were the failures of my three marriages, the deaths of family members, the financial difficulties, and the deep depressions and mood swings in addition to the ADD that made school so difficult for me. And that isn't even mentioning going bald at thirty years old!

I have struggled to learn how to deal with adversity in my life. I've gotten a little better at it. One thing you learn playing pro football is how to accept failure. During my 14-year career, for example, I threw 212 touchdown passes, thank you very much—and had 210 passes intercepted. Including the postseason and Super Bowl, I threw 242 touchdown passes—and 236 interceptions. That means that 236 times in my career—imagine that, 236 times—I took the snap from my center, dropped back to pass, looked around—and then did the very worst thing possible for a quarterback to do. I threw the ball to the other team. My goodness. I threw so many interceptions that I used to make special guest appearances in head coach Chuck Noll's nightmares.

Throwing an interception was always easy for me. I'll never forget my rookie year in Pittsburgh, the sportswriters were just brutal to me. Bradshaw should be like the Pirates' Willie Stargel, they wrote; he got a hit one out of every three times at bat. So one Sunday I came to the sidelines after throwing an interception and Chuck said, "You're killing me, you're killing me. You've only completed thirty-five percent of your passes."

I said, "What's the problem with that? At least that's half!"

I hated interceptions. Absolutely hated them. I felt humiliated, embarrassed. A complete failure. Would you hire a plumber who solved half of all your plumbing problems? Would you go to a lawyer who lost half his cases? Would you go to a doctor who was 100 percent right only 50 percent of the time?

In college if a pass was intercepted I would get so angry I'd lose control of myself. I remember getting so mad one time when a small defensive back intercepted a pass I caught up with him and pushed him out of bounds—then I picked him up and body-slammed him and broke his collarbone. As I matured as a quarterback I learned how to handle it better—mostly because I had 236 opportunities to practice responding to having a pass intercepted.

It took me a long time to learn how to deal with failure and adversity. I'm much better at it now; I don't throw my golf clubs near as far. When I was growing up my natural response when something went wrong was to hit something. That's what I was taught. My father had learned from his father that the best way to deal with problems was to use your head—basically as a battering ram. One summer day when I was about eight years old, for example, my brother Gary and I got chased home by three older, big kids—one of them was about 6 feet, 115 pounds—and ran into the safety of our basement. I admit, my friends, I was scared. I knew if my brother and I got in a fight with those kids there were only two possible outcomes: Either we were gonna get hurt, or we were gonna get hurt real bad.

My father found us there and asked what we were doing. Basically, we told him, saving our lives. "Hey," he said, "this ain't going to get it done. You're never gonna get anywhere running from people. So go get yourself those Little League baseball bats, they'll even up the sides. Then you go out there and settle this."

That was the day I learned the importance of standing up to my fears—with a baseball bat.

My solution to just about every problem was who do I hit. When we moved to Iowa the kids didn't like us one bit. We were Southerners, we were different. My mom took us to school and told us she would pick us up. After school we were leaning against a car, just waiting—being from the South we were experts on that particular subject—when a gang of kids surrounded us. What those kids did not know was that the blue jeans, shirt, and sneakers I had on were going to have to last all year. These were my serious clothes. I had a terrible decision for a young boy to make; who was liable to be tougher, a gang of ten kids—or my mother all by herself?

That was no contest. Those kids started pushing us around, stomping on our feet, they spit at us. But we didn't dare fight back. I leaned over and told Gary, "You just remember who all these people are. 'Cause I'm gonna kick every one of them's ass!"

And over that next year I did just that. That year I kicked me some prime Iowa behind. One by one I picked them off. After school. In the boys' room. I learned how to fight. I learned how to protect myself. I learned how to get hit. And I learned that I didn't have to resolve a problem right away. I could take my time and get it done.

Of course, I also learned that beating people up didn't make the problem go away. It just made those people angry. That didn't matter to me, though; I thought if I was just a little tougher I could solve my problems. I know it's hard to believe, looking at me now—the big old dog-petting, crying-at-movies hunk of love that I am—but for a long time my temper was out of control. I was in my front yard one afternoon, for example, throwing my football up on the roof and catching it as it came down. A couple of older kids from the neighborhood grabbed my football and tossed it across the highway in front of my house into a big patch of sandburs. Sandburs are nothing but little round balls of stickers. They're like natural Velcro, they stick to fabric and skin and they hurt. I didn't know how to get into that patch to get my ball back, but one of these kids helped me. He threw me right into it.

I came out of that patch covered with burs, I had stickers everywhere, mostly I looked like a human pom-pom. Eight years later I was still pulling out burs. Thinking about it still makes my skin crawl. But I went after that kid. I tried to kill him. I tackled him right on the highway and I was beating up on him. A truck driver stopped his eighteen-wheeler right in the middle of the road and pulled me off him.

My friends, if that truck driver hadn't come along there never would have been a *Calypso Christmas*. And I might have met Burt Reynolds for the first time when he made *The Longest Yard*—the story of a football game that takes place *inside* a prison. I could have been the technical advisor.

I wasn't a bad kid, I was a good kid with a bad temper. But being tough was the only tool I had to deal with adversity. I guess that was why I so loved playing football. Just imagine a kid like me discovering a game in which it is considered a good thing to smash the opposing player as hard as possible. Looking back, it was a very good thing that I grew up in the South. If there had been ice I might have played hockey: What a great game that would have been for me; you were allowed to smash into the opposing player as hard as you could—and they let you play with a big stick!

As I got older I also began throwing the javelin. Basically, the javelin is nothing more than a gentrified spear. Fortunately, by the time I learned how to throw that spear I had gained some control over my emotions. Let me give you a bit of good advice: Never get in a fight with an angry javelin chucker.

Look, bad things happen to everybody, even good quarterbacks. If they didn't, we wouldn't need the entire insurance industry. And if we didn't have the insurance industry what would happen to all of the insurance salesmen in this country? So it's actually a good thing that bad things happen.

Every one of us has had to learn how to deal with adversity in our lives. Adversity comes in all forms and intensities. It ranges from sitting on an airplane for five hours next to an insurance salesman to death. In no particular order. No one is immune to it. Bad things happen to everybody, the important thing is how you deal with them. For example, I remember seeing a picture in the newspaper of a candidate for Congress from West Virginia rolling on the floor fighting with a reporter. The caption explained that the reporter had been interviewing the candidate and the fight erupted when he asked him, "Do you think your recent stay in a mental institution is going to hurt your campaign?"

Rule number one: Punching generally is not considered a good way of dealing with a difficult situation.

I started understanding how to really deal with rough situations when Steelers' coach Chuck Noll benched me. That was so long ago people were still referring to me as "The Blond Bomber." I wasn't playing well, the team wasn't winning, which to me still seemed like a pretty flimsy reason to put me down on the bench. But I was devastated. I'd sat on the bench in high school and college but that was because there was a quarterback ahead of me playing well. I'd never been given an opportunity to play and fail. I wasn't comfortable with failure. Rarely if ever in my life had I felt that depressed. It was just awful. I felt like I had personally disgraced every person who shared my DNA.

At that time pro football teams even had bad benches. Narrow and uncomfortable. I hated sitting on the bench so I made a decision: I wanted to be traded. I went into Chuck Noll's office to officially request a trade. I played for a lot of fine coaches in my career. From my high school coach, Lee Hedges, my coach at Louisiana Tech, Maxie Lambright, to Noll they had one thing in common, not one of them ever ended a discussion about a negative situation without giving me a positive outlook. They gave me hope that I could change the situation.

Chuck Noll put his head down and said nothing but wonderful things about me. He explained that he believed in me, he knew I had talent. He told me specifically what I needed to do to improve. "Be prepared, Terry," he told me. "Don't waste time feeling sorry for yourself. Don't disappear into a hole . . ."

When I left his office I had regained my confidence in myself. I was psyched! I was ready! Chuck Noll was right; I had the ability to be the very best benchwarmer he had ever had not playing for him!

What Noll really did was give me hope and remind me forcefully that it was within my own power to change the situation. Knowing that the only thing really permanent in my life is the hair on . . . the . . . skin on my scalp has been very important. Just about everything else is subject to real and immediate change. Definitely including my moods. There have been times in my life when I have been so depressed that I had to remind myself that I wasn't going to feel that bad for the rest of my life. Time heals, but when I'm depressed I just wish time didn't take so much time.

The fact is that when I was benched I took advantage of the situation to do the work I needed to do. I learned how to study the other team, I learned how to get the most out of practice, I learned how to prepare. So when I got the opportunity to play I felt well prepared.

As a player I always accepted the blame for my failures. When necessary I even accepted the blame for other people's failures: My fault, I shouldn't have thrown that pass to you while you were so wide open. But I never made excuses. When I sat on that bench I didn't blame the bench. The man who replaced me was "Jefferson Street" Joe Gilliam. Joe Gilliam was one man who could throw the football better than me; he had a stronger arm than I did. He was amazing. But he never accepted responsibility for his own actions. He was always making excuses. Once, I remember, he was two hours late for a quarterback meeting. Two hours. When Chuck asked him where he'd been, Gilly told him matter-of-factly that somebody had thrown paint on the hood of his Mercedes and he'd been busy all morning trying to get it off.

"That's tough," Chuck said, "Why don't we go outside and take a look at it."

They returned about ten minutes later. Chuck was really impressed. "Let me tell you all something," he said to us, "you guys ever need any touch-up work done on your car you ask Joe Gilliam where to go. These people did such a good job that car looks like it's never been touched!"

Another time Gilly got to practice late, he explained, because he'd driven his wife to the hospital and had to take a cab to the stadium from there—and the cab driver had gotten lost. Gotten lost? He couldn't find our ballpark, Three Rivers Stadium? It wasn't hard to find—it was right where the three rivers come together.

Joe Gilliam definitely could have been a star in the National Football League. He had the physical ability. What he didn't have was the emotional stability. When things started going bad for him he turned to alcohol and drugs. Contrary to all those reports, I am not naïve. I knew that players in professional football used drugs. But I never saw it. With me sitting on the bench Gilliam won four of six games, then he had an awful game against the Raiders. I got another chance to play and succeeded. Gilliam couldn't deal with it. A year later he was out of football. He got into hard drugs and lost everything. Everything.

I wish I could feel sorry for him, or people like him—but I can't, as cruel as it sounds. I liked him a lot, but I just don't feel sorry for anyone who throws away their career, their life, because of drugs. Instead I get angry about it. Doing drugs is incredibly selfish. When you choose to do drugs you're not considering the responsibility you have to your family, your friends, your employer, your team. There are so many people who would have given anything to have Gilly's talent, but he abused it. I wish I could be more sympathetic.

There have been times when I've felt sorry for myself.

Times I kind of wallowed in sorrow. I admit it, I have been a wallower. Hey, there's Terry, what's that he's doing?

Wallowing.

Wow, I never saw anybody wallow like that. You ever see anybody wallow that good?

Nope, never did.

My basic wallowing technique was to go deep, but not long. When something bad happened to me I got deep into it—but I tried hard not to stay down there too long. So maybe there is something good to be said about having an Attention Deficit Disorder, which makes it hard for me to stay focused on one thing: Oh, man, this is terrible, this is awful, I don't know if I'm ever going to get over this, is there any chocolate? What's on the TV?

Rule number two: Don't help make a difficult situation even worse by taking thoughtless actions. Remember the shepherd in the Bible who was so upset when one of his sheep wandered away that he went after it and lost his entire herd? Remember the farmer who had a beautiful daughter and one night a salesman—well, that's a completely different story.

Now didn't I tell you these rules were simple?

So how do you deal with adversity? That's a good question, thank you for asking Terry.

Years ago the Buffalo Bills had a fine place-kicker named Booth Lustig. Now, Booth Lustig believed in a form of mental positive reinforcement called psychocybernetics. The theory was that if you really concentrated and imagined yourself doing something perfectly over and over, your mind would stimulate the right muscles and when you actually did it you would perform better. One afternoon at practice a coach saw Lustig sitting by himself lost in some sort of daze. "Booth," he said, "what are you doing?"

Lustig looked right at him and said seriously, "Practicing."

You actually can learn quite a bit from professional athletes. Like where Three Rivers Stadium was before they tore it down, for example. (Note: IT WAS RIGHT BY THE THREE RIVERS!) But to be successful professional athletes have to be able to deal with both incredible highs and tremendous lows—happening within minutes of each other. The first thing any successful athlete knows is that you have to learn how to focus on the positive and try to eliminate the negative.

When I was playing I used a self-hypnotism technique taught to me by our strength coach Lou Reicke. I focused on three words: *relax, confidence, concentrate.* Focusing on those words allowed me to pretty much forget everything else, to block out negative thoughts. While you're welcome to borrow my three words, truthfully I think you can pick out your own words and focus on them—oh, for example, words like: *Bradshaw, money, send.*

I believe an athlete actually can talk himself or herself out of failure straight into success. Now please, that does not mean sweet-talking the officials. I'll tell the jokes here. Bad as they are. But if you listen carefully to an athlete being interviewed you can hear them preparing to be successful. Tiger Woods is always so calm, even when he isn't playing well. He says all the right things. "Even though I shot a ninety-four I hit enough good shots. I made a great putt on fourteen to save that triple bogey and it really got me going." The man focuses on his success, not his failure. It took me some time to learn that. At the beginning of my career when I threw an interception I got shaken. I focused on it. I saw it over and over in my head and it definitely affected my play the remainder of the game. So it wasn't just an interception, it was a failure that led to more failure.

Later in my career, after I'd had success with the Steelers, my anger would pass quickly. Hey, fans, that's the first interception I've thrown today and we've already played almost three whole minutes! Focus on the positive. That is applicable to anything you do. If you're trying to sell your product to a customer you don't tell them, "And just wait'll you meet our repairmen; they've had so much experience that whatever goes wrong they can fix." Of course you don't. You tell them that the only repairman the company had just one day upped and died of boredom.

Why do you take the advice of one stockbroker rather than someone else? Because he focuses on his success. "Oh yeah, I bought IBM for my clients when it was just I." Would you give that person your money if he begged you, "Please, please let me invest your money. No stockbroker in history has ever invested in fifty consecutive stocks that have lost money, so this time the law of averages is definitely with me."

Having a positive attitude will definitely help you overcome failure. Being a single man now, I enjoy meeting nice, attractive women. But I don't enjoy being rejected by them. So I developed a whole new attitude. When I see an attractive woman I say to myself, Terry, I'm positive she won't go out with you—and I save myself all that rejection.

There are some people who tell me I should cut down on that self-deprecating humor, but fortunately they are outnumbered by all those other people who respect my honesty.

It isn't enough just to talk about success, to use the words of success; you really have to believe in yourself. Chuck Noll used to call it "false chatter." He hated that yabba dabba do, we're gonna beat 'em, we're gonna smash 'em, we're gonna make 'em use the expensive long-distance service rather than 10-10-220!

Chuck loved those people who went about their business quietly. Chuck's attitude always reminded me of the great scene from *Indiana Jones* in which a swashbuckling sword waving karate-killing thug stands in front of Harrison Ford and yips and yaps and screams and threatens and shows him every great martial arts move in history. Indiana Jones just stands there watching quietly. Just waiting, dum-de-dum-dum, and when that man finally pauses—Indy takes out his gun and shoots him.

Indiana Jones definitely could have played for Chuck Noll with that attitude—and with that gun. That's why I love it when football players score a touchdown and rather than going Rockette they just drop the ball in the end zone or hand it off to somebody. Their attitude is simply cool: I've been here before, I'm not surprised I'm here now, and I will be back in the future. In fact, I like it here so much I may just decide to live here.

I like that as opposed to: I scored a touchdown! A touchdown! Me! Oh my goodness gracious sakes alive I can't believe it can you believe it I can't believe it I am so excited I want the whole world to know I did it all by myself with only the help of these other ten guys!

I can't even imagine what it's like to be Tiger Woods, who

expects to win every tournament in which he plays. He doesn't hope he is going to win, the man knows it. He is probably surprised when he doesn't win. The fact is that most people aren't surprised by failure, they're prepared for it, on some level they even expect it. That's the Oh, man, I knew that was going to happen, syndrome. I knew that customer was going to decide he didn't want to buy a plaid refrigerator. I knew that the woman I love secretly really wanted to date a Sherpa.

Rule number three: A positive attitude will definitely make it easier for you to deal with adversity.

But generally it isn't enough. Early in my pro career when I was having a bad day I would start experimenting. Hmmm, throwing the football overhand isn't working, let me drop down a little and see if I can wing it sidearm. When that failed I tried something else: Left-handed, that's it, I'll try throwing it with my left hand! I was fourth-guessing myself.

All athletes experience that. One day a shooting guard will make every shot; on the same court the very next day he can't hit the rim. A batter suddenly goes into a slump. I've played the same golf course under generally the same conditions many times—yet I've scored differently every time.

There is a reason that this happens. I mean, there has to be, right? But I don't know what it is. I'm not going to lie to you about that, that would be silly—I'm going to save my lies for more important things. What I do know is that when things start going wrong we all immediately start looking for new answers. Shoot the basketball differently. Make that sales pitch differently. Comb those long strands of hair way over the top of my poor bald head differently. We get far away from doing what we know how to do.

That makes no sense. I spent years learning how to throw a football accurately. Growing up I'm certain I threw at least one hundred thousand passes. I could throw a football so hard and accurately that if a car drove by going less than forty miles an hour with both the passenger and driver's windows open I could throw through that—well, maybe, I'm exaggerating, but I had spent more hours of my life throwing a football than doing any other single thing. My ability to throw the football long and accurately made me an all-American in college, a number-one draft choice in professional football, and the quarterback of the Pittsburgh Steelers. Folks, I could throw a football.

But if I threw a few poor passes in a row I decided, well, I guess that old method doesn't work anymore, maybe it's time to try something new. And I would try other things. And everything I tried just got me more confused and made the situation worse. I'm sure the same is true for many of you. This is very important: It has taken you your entire life, every single second of it from the instant you were born, to get to this very moment.

You may want to reread that sentence.

You've enjoyed some success in your personal life and your professional life, you've done things your way that have worked out pretty well. But as soon as you're faced with adversity you start doubting everything you know how to do. If I started a game badly, doubts crept into my mind; if I continued to play poorly, insecurity banged down the door of my mind; and if I couldn't make corrections, negative thoughts—negative thoughts took control. Like everybody else, I forgot those things that had worked for me in the past. I got away from what I knew.

I was very fortunate, I had coaches who were being paid

the big bucks to tell me not to do the same thing differently. They were pretty definite about it too. It was their job to make sure I did the same thing every time, that I got back to the basic mechanics. Throwing a football had become second nature to me, like getting turned down for dates. I didn't need to think about it; so when I did think about it I got mixed up. Pitchers don't think about their delivery. Basketball players don't have to think about their jump shots. The problem was that when things started to go wrong I began searching for solutions, and I got away from doing what came naturally; from doing what I had learned to do by practicing and playing the game for two decades; from doing what had worked well enough for me to be playing professional football. As I learned, maybe the most important thing I could do to overcome my problems was simply to go back to what I'd been doing successfully.

Simple, but universally applicable. If you've got a successful Italian restaurant and business slows down, you don't start selling Chinese food. There is no such thing as really good Italian Chinese food.

If your car engine starts making strange sounds you don't try to replace it with a bigger engine; you want it fixed and working normally.

If your husband or wife starts making strange sounds you don't try to replace them with a bigger—well, I guess there are always some people who want a bigger engine.

That's why I so admired athletes who could come out of the locker room after playing poorly in the first half and have a great second half. People who can recover from a bad start are the champions of life.

That's rule number four: The best thing to do when facing a problem is to go back to the basics. Vince Lombardi, one of the greatest coaches in football history, was asked after his Green Bay Packers lost two games in a row, what he was going to do to get back on track, to turn that team around. "I'll tell you what we're going to do," he said, "we're going to go back to basics." Tom Landry—maybe the greatest of all coaches, the creator of the 4–3 defense, four down linemen, three linebackers; the creator of the safety blitz—was a genius, but when things went bad for his Cowboys and reporters asked him what he intended to do about it, Landry with that stoic look in his eyes and his fine Christian principles said, "Young man, let me tell you something. We're gonna get back to basics." After winning four Super Bowls the Steelers started losing and reporters said to Chuck Noll: Joe Greene's done, Lambert's finished, Bradshaw's injured, what are you going to do about it?

I'm going to Disneyland! Chuck said. No he did not. He told them, "We're going back to where we started. Back to basics." That's what he said.

In San Francisco one day Joe Montana, the legendary Joe Montana, had a bad game; he only threw for 480 yards and five touchdowns—but he had an interception! After the game reporters raced into coach Bill Walsh's office, where he was sipping on a glass of char-do-ney and asked him what he intended to do to get Montana back on track. "Welllllll," he said softly, "I believe we shall return to the basics of the game of football."

As we like to cliché in sports, If you don't dance with the girl whut brung you, you're probably gonna get your toes stepped on a lot and that really hurts. Specially that pesky little toe.

Now let us review: When something unpleasant happens in your life, One: Don't hit. Two: Don't chase one sheep. Three: Remain positive. Four: Do what you know how to do best and watch out for that little toe.

Those are the rules: Take them or leave them. There is no instant replay in publishing.

CHAPTER 3

THE NOT-SO-SECRETS OF HAPPINESS

THE HAPPIEST TIMES OF MY LIFE WERE THE SUMMERS I spent with my family in Hall Summit, Louisiana. The entire family would stay together on my pawpaw's place. I remember most of all the comfort that came from just being with family. But I also remember that it was hot. I mean, it was hot. How hot was it?

Thank you for wondering; I'll tell you, it was so hot that the flies preferred to walk. In that heat it seemed like everything slowed down, even time. Saturday nights were my favorite time of the week. That's when the men would go on down to Slim's Barber Shop to get our hair cut. We went every Saturday whether we needed it cut or not. We'd sit around that barber shop listening to the men telling their hunting and fishing lies and family stories while the Grand Ole Opry was playing on the radio. "Howww-De!" Minnie Pearl would sing, and talk about her own family, "We took Brother to Nashville to try and get him a job. A man offered him thirty dollars a week and told him in five years he'd get two hundred. Brother told him that was fine, he'd be back in five years."

It was such a simple time. It was a time before money had begun to play a role in my life. I didn't know anything about money. My idea of wealthy would be my grandmother's brother's son. He was a wonderful man who owned a big farm. We would ride over to his house on an old dirt road and he would serve steaks for dinner. Steaks! He served steaks and it wasn't even a holiday. That's how rich he was. I remember one day he took all the kids to the store—he let us ride in the back of his truck, which was pretty exciting—and bought us a whole case of soda pop. I couldn't believe it; he could afford to buy the entire case of soda pop at one time. To me, that was pretty much the definition of rich.

I own a horse ranch in Texas and another one in Oklahoma. I got a lake on each spread. I got cars, I got big screen TVs; if I really wanted to I could buy a whole bottling plant worth of soda. I have earned a lot of money. And if there is one thing I truly regret it's the fact that I cannot enjoy my life. I appear to enjoy it. And I do have a good time. I work with nice people, I get to travel to wonderful places, and I have a job—several jobs—that I enjoy which don't involve being run down by a 330-pound lineman who doesn't know the meaning of the word *mercy*, and a lot of other words too! But the truth is that to afford those material things that bring me pleasure I have to spend most of my life away from them. At best I get to spend two or three days in a row at my ranch, then I'm off to a hotel room somewhere.

I could live very happily without the ranches, without the horses, the cars, without all of it. It probably wouldn't even make me too sad to see all of it go. I am not someone who has ever been possessed by my own possessions. I don't need a big house and I don't need a fancy car. For too many people the size of their house is inversely proportional to the amount of time they get to spend in it. They have put themselves in a position where they spend their life working hard to buy things that they never get time to enjoy because they're working so hard.

Most of us, including me, too often take the really important things in life for granted. We don't really recognize the things that make a difference in our lives. Many people come to my ranch and see the house and the horses and the lake and are overwhelmed by it. When I go to Hawaii I cannot stop staring at the ocean and the meadows of pineapples and the gorgeous mountains and the island doves and the beautiful people and I'm overwhelmed by it. I find myself telling Hawaiians, "You don't really appreciate what you have, do you?"

And they tell me, "It's nice, but it's not as nice as a horse ranch in Texas." Okay, maybe they don't actually say that. What they do say is, "It's home." Just like I say it. So maybe the best place to start is to look at your own life and appreciate those things that really matter; someone to love, your family, good health, your friends.

It's nice to have nice things. Anyone who tries to tell you that money doesn't matter in life really means it doesn't matter in *your* life. Money definitely does not guarantee happiness—I know many people who have a lot of money who aren't very happy—what money can do is make life a little easier. But in the top-ten list of the happiest days of my life, "cashing a check" does not appear.

Let me ask you this question: How many of you people reading this book right now would like to know how to double—I said double, my friends—the amount of money you have in the bank? How to guarantee that you would never have to worry about having enough money again? How to have more money than you ever dreamed possible?

I can practically hear you singing, Amen to more money than we ever imagined, brother Terry, Amen.

Of course you want to know. Well, me too! Who wouldn't? Believe me, if I knew that you'd be saying "'Member that guy Terry Bradshaw we used to see all over the TV? Whatever happened to him? After he got all that money we never heard from him again." But as I've already explained, I don't have the answers. I do know that in just about everybody's life money causes considerable problems. There are probably more women in this world who want to date me for my good looks than there are people who feel they have just enough money to make them happy. How much money is enough? That's an easy question to answer: Just a little more than you have.

No matter how much money you have, or don't have, the problems we all face are pretty much the same. I work to meet a payroll, support my kids, pay the mortgage on my house, pay the mortgage on my third former wife's divorce attorney's house. And the fears are the same too: What am I gonna do if I can't make the bills this month?

Admittedly in my case the bills are probably a little bigger than for many other people. When you don't have money the problems are obvious and extreme: food and shelter. But in my case in addition to paying the rent, child support, all the bills, and my personal expenses, I have substantial business expenses. There are a lot of people who depend on me keeping the Circle 12, my horse ranch, in operation. And it is expen-

46

sive. Believe me, people who tell you money "ain't hay" have never had to pay for hay. I'm responsible for the livelihood of all the people who work on the ranch. It's a responsibility I take seriously. It's a commitment. I have to be away from the ranch just to pay for the ranch.

My parents used to say our family was rich in love, which was another way of saying we weren't rich in money. I began learning the value of money when I was three years old and staged my first and only robbery. I went with my mother to visit a good friend of hers. I remember it was raining that day. As my mother and this woman socialized I played in the back of the house—and in the back bathroom I found a whole jar of money. Oh, my goodness gracious, I had never seen so much money untended in the entire three years of my life. There were pennies and nickels, I don't know how much money it was, it could have been as much as one dollar. That jar was just singing my name, "Terrrrr—ry, Terrrrr—ry." Yes, Jar? "Take me home with you."

Well how could I resist? I took all that money and put it in my pocket. The Bradshaw family fortune was beginning to build. I got away with it clean too, at least until I got home and my mother the detective found it in my pocket. "Terry, where did you get that money?" She definitely did not sing my name.

I was three years old, I wasn't allowed out of the house without permission, so there were a limited number of alibis open to me. "I don't know, Mommy," I said earnestly. This probably would have been a very good time for me to raise the subject of miracles.

"Don't you lie to me, Terry. Where did you get that money?"

47

I was sticking to my alibi, "I don't know, Mommy." I smiled broadly. I was playing the "cute" defense.

Nobody ever makes bank robbers bring the money back to the bank. But my mother put me back in the car, took me back to that woman's house, and made me hand it to her. "I found this," I said.

"Terry . . ." my mother warned.

"In my pocket," I admitted. I got a Momma-whipping that day, which while not as bad as a Daddy-whupping was definitely bad enough.

Everyone in my family worked hard, following the example of my father. When I was growing up he always had chores for us. The one we probably hated most was clearing out his vegetable garden. The thing about that garden was as we grew bigger so did his garden. I had an assortment of jobs growing up, not one of them requiring more brains than muscle. I did everything from hauling skids on a pipeline to selling used cars.

I never had an allowance. To earn money I mowed yards for a dollar a yard. One year I worked on my hands and knees digging weeds out of a football field for $42 a week. With my first week's pay I went down to the clothes store because they were having a sale on rayon short-sleeved shirts. There was a big stack of them right in the middle of the table. They were selling for fifty cents, and I bought every one of them that fit me. That was my very first purchase. I was so proud of those shirts because I had never in my life had anything so nice. They were nice too, right up until you wore them. Then they fell apart. The first time you washed them the strings came loose. When I put one on for the second time I looked like I was wearing a ball of string.

I worked in a clothing store on Saturdays. I was a machine welder on drill stem pipes. One summer I hauled hay. In college when I came home for Thanksgiving and Christmas vacations I worked all week building doors at a window and door manufacturing plant for $1.75 an hour. I worked ten hours a day six days a week. There was no paying job beneath my dignity.

My rookie year in the National Football League I was paid $25,000. For me, that was a fortune. The most money I'd ever had in the bank at one time before that was $350, which I saved for college and had lasted me an entire year. I didn't know anything about handling money; I especially didn't know about taxes. I had never even filed a tax return. But at the end of the year a CPA told me I had to pay the government $7,200. I had $7,000 in the bank. So to earn money during the off-season I took a job at Bill Hannah Ford selling used cars. All my friends would come to see me and I'd give them the same deal I wished someone would give me. I gave them the deal of a lifetime. I may still hold the all-time record for most used cars sold without making any profit. As a salesman I had a selling technique probably best described as "seriously pathetic."

Even after I became more successful with the Steelers I wasn't about to give up my summer job. I never knew when I might chance upon another pile of rayon shirts and I wanted to be ready to pounce. When I did begin to gain some recognition I began appearing in commercials for the used car lot. If anybody ever asks you just how much you would embarrass yourself to earn a paycheck, I suggest you thoughtfully look up into the sky, rub your jaw between your thumb and forefinger and say, a whole lot, but probably not as much as Terry Bradshaw.

For one commercial I actually dressed up like a mountain hillbilly. I had the beard, the hat, the cornpone pipe. My dad had an old dilapidated shack on his farm and we filmed it there. I was supposedly sitting inside reading the newspaper when suddenly something I read shocked me. My jaw dropped open, I stood up, flung open the door—which immediately fell off its hinges—and yelled, "Clyde, lookee here. Bill Hannah Ford has an 'If you can push, pull or tow your old car in they'll give you somethum' for it.'" Two people were crouching inside under the window frames and when I opened the door they started throwing chickens out the windows. Oh, man, those chickens were petrified; they came flying out the window right into the camera as I was trying to remember my lines.

Winning four Super Bowls has made a significant difference in my life. Now instead of doing commercials with chickens I work with a puppet named Alf.

There hasn't been a time in my life when I haven't had at least one job. When I started earning a reasonable salary I decided that I needed to invest for the future. There were a lot of young divorce lawyers graduating from law school who were going to be depending on me. But truthfully I didn't know anything at all about investing. In fact, I knew so little about investing that as my first major investment I bought myself a brand-new boat.

I'll just wait right here, right at this comma, until all you boat owners stop laughing. When I got drafted I bought a life insurance policy. That was not meant to be a comment on the quality of the Steelers' offensive line, the people who would be protecting me, it was just that I thought buying life insurance was what all adults did. The way I understood this policy was that if I died I would be a very rich man.

Then somebody told me to invest in the commodities market, invest in futures, they said. Well, that definitely made more sense to me than investing in the past. Linebacker Andy Russell was a graduate of the Harvard Business School, and he told me what to do. I bought some oil and gas stocks. I bought some Dr Pepper because that was my favorite brand. I probably owned less than five hundred shares of that stock, but every time I drank a bottle of Dr Pepper I felt like I was being loyal to my own company.

But primarily I invested in land. Once, when asked for investment advice, Mark Twain recommended investing in land "because they're not making it anymore." More important, as every real estate broker knows, it isn't going to cost any less either. When I started buying land I very quickly learned the language of real estate. I found out what all those real estate expressions really mean. A lot, for example. I always thought a lot was—a lot. But one thing "a lot" isn't, for example, is a lot. It's usually a lot less than a lot; it probably should be called "a little." One time a real estate broker was showing me some expensive farmland and I said, "That's not a lot of land, is it?"

He agreed with me. "You're right," he said. "It's almost twenty lots."

You know that expression *dirt cheap*? Well, dirt isn't cheap. Dirt can be expensive, and the more fertile the dirt the more it is going to cost.

And you know why the person who sells you lots is known as a real estate broker? That's because by the time you're finished doing business with him you're going to be a lot broker than you ever thought possible. A lot, in this sentence, meaning—a lot.

The only good investment I ever made on my own was buying a ranch in Louisiana. There is considerable competition for the worst investment I ever made. But I would have to admit that my ostrich egg venture certainly would be among the finalists. I was going to be to ostriches what Frank Perdue is to chickens: a mass murderer. Several years ago it seemed like everyone was talking about ostrich meat. Well, okay, maybe not in your neighborhood. But the rumor was that ostrich meat was going to become very popular. It was tasty, low in fat, high in protein. It was the perfect product for diet- and health-conscious America.

Man, that still sounds promising. So I decided I was going to become an ostrich farmer, Terry the ostrich king. I could almost hear people saying with awe, "Wow, Terry, you got the biggest ostrich I have ever seen. Boy, Terry, love your ostrich." I had four hundred acres of God's beautiful earth just needing to feel life. I had visions of a great herd of ostriches—doing whatever it is ostriches do—all over my land. I had been a cattleman, now I was going to be an ostrichman.

Lemme have an amen for ostriches, people.

So I bought a pair of ostriches. Truthfully, it wasn't exactly a pair of ostriches. It was a pair of future ostriches. Actually, I bought two ostrich eggs. I thought I got a great buy on them too, I only paid $7,000 for them. This is the truth, I paid $7,000 for two bird eggs. So, my friends, if anyone ever asks you who the greatest salesman in history is, you just sit quietly waiting until everybody else has had their say and then you tell them, "How about the guy who sold two bird eggs to Terry Bradshaw for $7,000?" Or when things are really going bad around the office; when your biggest customer is unhappy and the important shipment is late and those pictures they took of you in the stockroom at last year's Christmas party show up on the corporate web site, you just lean right back and think, could be worse, could be a lot worse. I could have paid $7,000 for two ostrich eggs like Terry Bradshaw.

When I finally got my two eggs I didn't even know what to do with them. I certainly wanted to protect my investment, but I wasn't going to sit on them. I wasn't going to put them in a safe deposit box. Let's be honest here, if God had intended ostriches to be raised in Texas he wouldn't have invented shotguns.

I definitely should have known better. When was the last time you opened a restaurant menu and saw they were serving poached ostrich? How many ostrich cookbooks are there on the market? What's your favorite ostrich recipe? When was the last time anybody served ostrich steaks and Dr Pepper? There is a reason for this: Normal people don't eat filet of ostrich.

Finally I went to the man who sold me these eggs and told him they were killing my investment portfolio. I had some shares of IBM, of Xerox, I had my Dr Pepper stock, Red Man Tobacco, and I had these two bird eggs. He agreed with me that not every man is well suited for ostrich ranching and agreed to return my money. I didn't even get to name my eggs.

I've learned that money does not bring me satisfaction. Mostly it brings with it the need to make more money. I gave a speech to a group of young people and their parents in Oklahoma. I said to them that the real joy in life is life, living life day to day; you just have to be smart enough and aware enough to appreciate it. The good and the bad. It's no secret. It's no more complicated than that. Too many people spend too many years of their lives trying to reach a goal only to discover when they finally get there that the real joy is taking the journey.

We are all on this journey, this incredible journey. There is nothing that stimulates the mind of a human being more than a journey. We all want to take that trip, we all want to know what's going to happen around the next corner. It's the most exciting adventure of your life—because it is your life.

During most of my football career I was too busy playing football to appreciate the privilege of playing football. I'm sure most people believe that the most enjoyable moments of my career were winning four Super Bowls. But that's not true. That part of my career that brought me the greatest pleasure were the years when we were building a great team. Position by position I could see the Steelers getting better and better, preparing to win. When I started I struggled in football. I failed, I failed often, but I learned a little more each week and gradually I became a pretty good quarterback. And gradually the team started winning. Finally we made it to our first play-off game. We didn't know if we could win at that level until we won. Then we went to a championship game and finally to a Super Bowl. It took a long time to get there and it required a lot of hard work; we had to confront a lot of self-doubts, a lot of insecurities, a lot of bad breaks. We had to believe in Chuck Noll's plan. And all that time I was so focused on getting to the future that I forgot to enjoy the present. I was so focused on reaching the summit that I neglected to appreciate the beauty of the climb.

The great joy in winning the Super Bowl was magnified because it had all those building years wrapped into it, that's what made it so special. The journey. The trip. Same thing in the horse business. If my dream was owning a world-champion stallion I could go to the bank, borrow the money, and buy a world-champion stallion. But what would be the joy in that? It would bring me no satisfaction. About the only thing I could do would be take people over to my barn and say, "Look at my world champion. Ain't he a beauty!"

But then somebody might say, "Wow, Terry, you raised him?"

"Heck no, I bought him. But I raised the money to buy him!" That would bring me no satisfaction at all.

But if I could answer, "Oh yeah, I raised his momma and I bred her to this other horse I raised and I remember the day she dropped and then there was the time he had that little bout with colic but he came through . . ."

If I could answer it that way it would bring me incredible satisfaction. Just let me point out to you that the Declaration of Independence identifies the basic human rights as life, liberty, and the pursuit of happiness—not the pursuit of money. I have been diligently pursuing happiness my whole life. On many occasions I've caught it, but it just keeps getting away. What I have learned during that pursuit is that I don't find my personal happiness in those things money can buy.

Actually there are a lot of things that bring me happiness; most important, being with my girls, Rachel and Erin. I'd like to say that as a father I'm a tough disciplinarian; I would definitively like to say that but it wouldn't be true. I'm about as tough as Jell-O with my girls. One time we went to the quarter horse competition in Columbus, Ohio. Erin was showing in the youth class. But while I was looking at horses they followed a sign that pointed them in the direction of puppies.

I warned them before I let them go that I was not going to get them a puppy. Each of them had animals at both my house and their mother's house. I had dogs and horses and cats, I just didn't have room for any more animals. About an hour later they came running up to me all excited. "Oh, Dad," Erin said, "we found the most beautiful puppy . . ."

We are not getting another puppy.

". . . and you ought to see it, Dad, and it's so beautiful, Dad, and you'd love it so much, Dad, and we told the lady that we were your daughters and she told us that she hadn't intended to sell this puppy, Dad, she wanted to keep it to breed and raise it herself because it is so special, but because it's you, Dad, she'll let us buy it. Dad, you have to come see this puppy."

We are not getting . . .

I held out for maybe another hour. All you parents know how tough this situation can be. It's a good opportunity to teach children the most important lessons in life: You say "Daddy" in the right tone and you can have anything you want. I explained logically why we couldn't buy this dog. I laid it out for them clearly and rationally. But I had no chance, I was being attacked by the worst of all combinations: a salesman, my daughters, and a puppy.

I agreed to look at this puppy. They grabbed my hands— "Com'on, Daddy"—and we walked six hundred yards up a hill.

As we got closer they let go and took off running. I reached in my wallet and pulled out four hundred-dollar bills, hoping it wouldn't cost me any more than that.

Three hundred, the puppy salesman said. This was a pure-bred corgi, he added, suggesting that I think of it as an investment.

No, ostrich eggs were an investment. This was simply me caving in to my daughters. I couldn't resist, they'd called me "Daddy." We took it back to the hotel. The girls promised me they would take care of this dog forever, or twenty minutes, whatever came first. This dog was so happy to be coming home with us that she peed all over the carpet. Her name is Sammy. She does all these little things to endear herself to me, like ripping up my very expensive carpet.

So my daughters bring me happiness. Animals bring me happiness. I've learned good lessons from animals. Animals don't demand anything from you. They never ask to borrow your car, complain about the weather, or charge movies on your pay-TV. The sweeter and gentler and kinder and more respectful you are to an animal, the more it will respond to you. Many times I've stepped into the stall of a nervous horse and just squatted there; I have literally stayed still in a stall for more than an hour and eventually that horse understood that I was not there to hurt him, and came over to me and nuzzled me. Horses have what's known as "horse sense." It means horses understand one of the basic rules of happiness: Be nice to me, I'll be nice to you. Most living things respond real well to a kind hand. What could be simpler than that, my friend?

But I warn you, don't try that behavior at home with someone you love. Trust me, you try walking into a room and squatting down in a corner without saying a word and I guarantee you it will inevitably lead to three questions: Why are you squatting in the corner? What's wrong with you? Are you completely out of your mind? That's what is known as "nonsense."

I don't ride horses. This is not due to any strongly held belief about the exploitation by man of the noble beast, it's just that I have a bad back and it hurts too much when I ride. Riding is therapeutic for some people, not me. I get my enjoyment from walking amongst my horses, loving on them, hugging on them, watching them interact with other horses. Every horse is different, physically and temperamentally. Some don't want you to touch their ears. Some don't want you to touch their nose. You learn these traits when you pick yourself up off the ground. When we buy a horse I always ask the owner, does he have any bad habits.

Yessir, he does, Mr. Bradshaw, he smokes too much and hangs out with the mares all night.

I love my dogs. When I sit down in my big chair my dogs fight over my attention. Including Sammy. My dogs think I'm special and they can't even bark the words *Super Bowl*. All they want me to do is pet them and let them know that I love them. And I can express that with the palm of my hand. Dogs are not impressed by status. Find your dogs a filthy fireplug and they're happy. They communicate with other dogs by pee-mail. Remember this: Dogs get to see you naked—and they still like you!

Of course, I don't know if any of this is true concerning ostriches. But I can tell you from experience that ostrich eggs don't make good pets.

Close friends bring me happiness. The great game of golf on occasion brings me happiness. Lake fishing makes me really happy; I'm a catch-and-release man, which definitely makes the fish happy. Reading my Bible makes me very happy. The quiet of the early morning brings me happiness, that time when there's nothing going on, when I can make some coffee, sit down and just be. Winning a football game always made me happy, even if personally I hadn't played well; but playing well when we lost did not make me happy. There are a lot of things that make me truly happy; a pretty lady with a smile, kind words from people who know my work—whatever that is, exactly—old people holding hands just crushes me; and most important of all, just being with my family. And not one of these things requires a substantial amount of money. Not one.

I don't know what it is that makes other people happy. In my life the evidence is particularly strong that I definitely don't know what makes a wife happy. That is something each person has to determine for themselves. For some people happiness is a big car, a big house, big toys, the material things. There's nothing wrong with that. Some people catch fish and hang them up on a wall, showing people how proud they are that they outsmarted a fish.

My friends, and by this page you are my friends, happiness is where you find it. Just don't spend so much time looking for it that you miss what's right in front of you. In all the years I played pro football, only once, in the last minutes of my final Super Bowl when we had the game won, did I actually stop and take time to look around and savor the moment.

I have earned a lot of money, and much of it has gone to

make other people happy. Sometimes people stop in front of my ranch and they see the beautiful house, the barns and the horses, the lake and the pasture; my oh my, they must say, that boy Bradshaw has done good for himself.

But most times what they don't see is me—because I'm usually on the road earning money to pay for it all. And what they don't see are my girls because they're living with their mother down the road.

It really is very simple: Stop, take time to look around, and savor this moment.

CHAPTER 4

THE HEART HAS A HEART OF ITS OWN
AND OTHER DISASTERS

I REMEMBER THE FIRST TIME I HAD SEX.

Now that I have your complete attention I want to discuss a problem that I believe I share with all men: All women. Too often in my life in the war between the sexes I have been classified a noncombatant. Admittedly that was not my choice; it was more like by unpopular demand. But a lot of the problems that I've had to face were looking right back at me.

Dealing with women is much tougher than playing football. In football half of the game is defense. In fact, you can win a football game by playing good defense. In life there is no defense against women. Most of the really bad decisions I've made, decisions that have cost me dearly both emotionally and financially, have concerned my relationships with women. I suspect that relationships between men and women have been the source of more joy and unhappiness than anything else in our lives. This is one subject I can speak about as an expert: I've been married and divorced three times, each divorce being more painful than the last one. And I am willing to take responsibility for my part in those divorces, but I also blame my former wives. They married me.

I really do remember the first time I had sex.

Just checking to make sure you're still paying attention. The truth is I've always liked girls, I've just never been quite sure what to do with them. I remember my first loves, puppy loves. All I did was stare at them, hoping maybe they knew what to do. But something deep inside me made me want to impress them, show off my talents for them. I wanted to prove to them that I was definitely the most sophisticated nine-year-old on the entire block. Here's how mature I was: I could ride my bike with no hands.

Not that I had any place in particular to put those hands, of course.

Mary Alice Crawford was one of my first girlfriends. Besides her being an adorable redhead, I think what really appealed to me was that she lived right around the corner and had a trampoline in her backyard. My mother used to send my brother and me to the grocery store on our bikes, and I pedaled right by Mary Alice Crawford's house. One time I was carrying a loaf of sliced bread and a basket of strawberries, gliding down a steep hill, when I saw Mary Alice and a friend walking along. Well—this was my opportunity to show off for my best girl. I took my hands off the handlebars, tucked that bread under my arm and started pedaling. I never did notice that patch of sand alongside the road. As I turned to wave to Mary Alice my bike hit that patch. The bike slid right out from under me. I went flying, then hit that concrete road and started bouncing. I skimmed across that road like a thin rock on a flat lake. Pieces of bread were tossed everywhere. I had squashed strawberry all over my clothes. I was scratched and bleeding. I was hurting.

But I jumped right up. I knew Mary Alice had seen the whole thing. I'm okay, I'm okay. I'm fine. No big deal to a tough guy like me. I gave a little wave to Mary Alice. I picked up as many slices of bread as I could salvage, got the last few strawberries back into the basket, straightened the handlebars on my bike and rode away with another little wave. Dum de dum, bye Mary Alice, dum de dum, dum de dum . . .

I dum de dummed until I got around the corner. When I was sure the girls couldn't see me I layed down in someone's yard and I started moaning and groaning. I was in pain from the fall and I was in future pain from what my mom was going to do when I handed her the bread. My only real hope was that in her anger she'd mistake squashed strawberries for blood.

I suspect I realized it then that when it comes to women, men are just born stupid. And then it gets worse.

The Bradshaw boys were nice looking and polite. There were some girls who liked us, and naturally we liked being liked by them. It felt good. I even had a young lady from the neighborhood come knocking on my front door one Saturday morning, and, my friends, this was long before women pursued men. This had all the makings of a neighborhood scandal.

That made me feel great. She was a tomboy, but very cute. I figured I'd play hard to get. I shouted back at her through the screen that I was busy. But she was insistent. She wanted to see me. Man, Terry, I thought, you have got it! You have got the secret!

"Terry Bradshaw," she told me, "you come on out right

now, y'hear. I just bet my friend I could outrun you. So you just better get out here and race me."

Outrun me? A girl outrun me? I don't think so. I casually ambled out into the backyard. Even at that age I knew the stakes were pretty high: my reputation for the rest of my life. I could almost hear the conversation: Ole Terry just celebrated his ninetieth birthday. Never did get over losing that race to a girl.

Our backyard was about eighty yards long. We drew a line in the dirt, crouched down and took off. I was moving, I was humpin'; unfortunately so was she. I barely beat her, but I did beat her. Kicked her butt. Showed her who was boss. Hey, you're talking future Hall of Famer here, how would it look written on my plaque: Won four Super Bowls after losing a race to a girl! I guess I taught her to mess with me.

And all of womankind has spent the next four decades getting even with me for that.

I was in third grade the first time I kissed a girl. Nancy Hubbard. Nancy and I were deeply in love; we were committed to each other for all eternity or lunchtime. I would spend time in school drawing hearts and writing inside, "TB + NH." I walked her home from school for lunch every day. It was out of my way, but she was definitely worth it. She had eyes like chocolate candy. There was a billboard sign on the ground near her house. One day, I remember, I just couldn't wait anymore. "Nancy," I told her, "I got a surprise for you today." We walked behind the billboard and I said, "Now close your eyes." She closed her eyes and I kissed her right on the mouth.

Things have never been the same since. It was—wow! It

was good. My heart was thumping away. My whole body felt alive. I felt parts where I didn't know I had parts. I just about passed out. I had actually kissed a girl. Oh, my goodness gracious, life is sweet. That's it, I thought, now I've done it all.

But by fourth grade I had fallen in love with Dorinda Shaw.

I remember the first time I went parking with a girl. I had been anticipating this for only sixteen or seventeen years. I had been thinking about it even before I knew what it was. We drove to a secluded spot and began kissing. And kissed. And kissed some more. That was real kissing, that wasn't third-grade kissing behind the billboard. While I had very little experience, I took to kissing easily. Unlike football, I already had all the equipment I needed. My date didn't know how to kiss either, but we learned together. We just kissed the heck out of each other.

That was the limit though. She wouldn't let me touch her below the waist. Or above the waist either. That was forbidden territory. I definitely loved kissing, and even if I had known then that I was on the direct path to years of heartbreak and pain, a financial beating, and a plaque in the Divorce Lawyers Hall of Fame, I still would have kissed her.

I really honestly do remember the first time I had sex. Truthfully, I was scared to death. I was so nervous my whole entire body was shaking. But fortunately I was all alone. So no one knew that. As I eventually learned, men generally experience only two real problems in dealing with sex: Having sex and not having sex. Other than that it's easy. Every man knows that's true. When I was growing up, when I wasn't thinking about sex I was . . . I was . . . well, I guess I was always thinking about it. That and throwing a football.

Women have always fascinated and intrigued and per-plexed me. I had my first real girlfriend through high school and into college. Penny Clarke. She did what we all want our partners to do; she made me feel real good about myself. This was long before I was a star football player, long before I played pro football, but she found value in me. We wanted to get married but our parents talked us out of it. We were too young, they told us. Wait until after college, they said. I'm still waiting.

I don't think getting married is very difficult. Staying mar-ried is the really hard part. After my third divorce my momma sighed and reminded me, "Remember what I told you, son, this is what happens when you marry outside the family."

I've told my two girls that when I was playing football I broke every bone in my body. I told them that at practice they used to bury me in the middle of the field up to my head and then beat me. They've seen most of the scars on my body. If I have to fill out a medical insurance form that asks for a list of "previous operations" I have to get extra paper. Maybe I haven't broken all the bones in my body, but I have broken them from head to toe, from my nose to my foot. I've probably had fifteen substantial operations. I've been knocked out, laid up, and carried off the field. Yet putting all that together, every last stitch, it does not even begin to equal the pain I've experi-enced in my relationships.

If it is true, as we were taught in football, that the more you practice something the better you get at it, then my next marriage is going to be a very good one—because I've had plenty of practice. I am truly ashamed of the fact that I have been divorced three times. My first marriage was to a former

Miss Teenage America, Melissa Babich. We had only known each other a few months. I think the only thing we really had in common is that we didn't love each other. What I did love, I think, was the fact that a former Miss Teenage America would be attracted to me. That was definitely pretty cool. Ah, shucks, I'd like you to meet my wife, Miss Former Teenage America Bradshaw.

Naturally she was a very pretty woman. She was the kind of woman that when we walked into a room together everybody would immediately start talking about me: "Look at those two. What in the world is she doing with him?"

Melissa is one of the nicest people I've ever married. But I married her mostly because I had a big fight with my brother. I had returned to Louisiana after my second season with the Steelers and just went off on him. I don't even remember what we fought about. My brother wasn't talking to me. My brother! I was depressed about the season and depressed about fighting with my brother. I just wanted to feel good again. I hadn't written this book yet so I didn't know about rule number two: Don't go taking thoughtless actions just to make yourself feel better temporarily.

I called Melissa and asked her to marry me. Basically, it pretty much came down to the fact that she didn't have any better plans for the rest of her life so she said yes. Some people have surprise birthday parties, we had a surprise marriage. Besides making me feel better, the main reason I was getting married was that it was easier than trying to get a date.

Six weeks later Melissa and I were getting married. We had a very small wedding—we had to because we didn't have time to get invitations printed. I remember walking down the aisle smiling at my parents and her parents, and thinking, Oh, my God, what in the world am I doing? I am definitely out of my mind.

And I think that was a sentiment shared pretty much by everybody there that day. There are times in all of our lives, my friends, when we suspect we are about to make a colossal blunder. You know what I mean: "I'll just turn this dinky little valve right here and I'll bet nothing's going to happen." Or, "I'm going to tell my boss what I really think about this idea of his because he's a good guy and he'll respect me for my honesty." And the classic, "Believe me, this is the best investment you're ever going to make."

That was my wedding. It did serve the purpose of helping me get over my depression about that fight with my brother. Because that was nothing compared to the depression I was feeling about this marriage. Inside, I was devastated. I was an emotional wreck. The whole thing was absolutely ridiculous, which naturally meant it was the perfect thing for me to do. When I read the stories in the newspapers, "Steelers Quarterback Marries Miss Teenage America," it seemed even crazier.

Melissa was a sweet person and this was not her fault. I was just born this way. Our marriage lasted about eighteen months. When we beat the 49ers to make the playoffs at the end of the next season I called her and told her I wasn't coming back home. I wanted a divorce. That was a tough word for me to say. My people just didn't get divorced. My father and mother had been born married to each other. They had met during World War II when my father was welding in a shipyard next to her father. But I had to do it, I just didn't love her.

My father told me to go and see her. I walked in the house

and collected the few clothes I had and left. Oh, man, it was sad. I didn't love her and when you're not in love with someone any little thing they do you hold against them: Do you have to brush your teeth so loudly? Did you really have to buy *two* new shoes?

I knew even less about getting divorced than I did about marriage. I can so easily remember the first time I said those three little words: She gets what!? I couldn't believe it. Divorce was much worse than buying a boat as an investment. The most fortunate thing about it all was that I didn't have anything, and she got it all. Fact is, though, she deserved it. I felt that I had misled her, so to escape some of that guilt I wasn't going to contest anything. Whatever she got, she truly deserved. And she didn't want anything more than what was right.

When it was finally settled I knew I could never go through an experience like that again. Marriage just wasn't worth the guilt, the shame, and the embarrassment. I decided that it would be a long, long time, if ever, before I got married again. I had learned from my mistake and I definitely did not intend to make that same mistake a second time. And then I met JoJo Starbuck.

I loved Art Rooney, the owner of the Steelers. He told me once, "What you need is a girl who knows how to milk a cow." Choosing a wife, he said, was like buying a racehorse, "Some are good on fast tracks, some are good on off tracks, and some are good on any kind of track."

Unfortunately, he didn't say anything about ice. The year Melissa and I got divorced was the same year I lost the starting quarterback job to Joe Gilliam. It was a terrible time in my life.

Just awful. I found myself spending time in bars drinking and meeting pretty women who were easily impressed by the fact I played pro football.

Who would really want to lead a life like that?

Put your hands down please. I know to a lot of men that might sound like a fantasy, but for me it was an escape. This was not a lifestyle I enjoyed. It wasn't really for me. I had been a Christian for so long—at least I thought I was—and I pulled away from it that year. Sometimes when you go back to pass and start looking around and realize all your receivers are covered, there is for an instant a feeling of helplessness before that desire for self-preservation kicks in. That's what I felt like. Like all my receivers of my life were covered and to survive I had to improvise.

One night I went with some teammates to see the *Ice Capades*. The star of the show was JoJo Starbuck, who had been a champion pair skater with her partner, Ken Shelley. She was lovely. The first time I saw her I remember thinking, wow, look at that absolutely gorgeous girl skating. That feeling was pretty much the high point of our relationship.

I wanted to meet her but I was pretty shy. What do you say to a beautiful ice skater, I like your figures? We spoke for a while, and it was obvious that she was attracted to me. Just one year later she called me right back. A year. An entire year. So much could have happened in that time. I could have even had another date. But as it turned out JoJo was also serious about her religion. After reading a story about me in a Christian magazine she called the Steelers office to get in touch with me.

When the *Ice Capades* returned to Pittsburgh my teammate

Moon Mullins and I went to the show. I think I probably fell in love with her that night. Afterwards, I went backstage, or "backice" and fell for her.

She seemed to be everything I wanted in a woman: a good Christian, a nice person, very pretty, and pretty much living on the road. She was working for a touring ice show; much of the year she lived in hotels. We really spent very little time together. I'd fly to meet her and watch her skate. JoJo knew as much about football as I did about ice skating. Before we'd met she had never even heard of me. And to me, ice skating was basically trying to stand up on ice.

It was definitely a whirlwind courtship. Three weeks after we met we were engaged. Three weeks. You can't get a plumber in three weeks, but I got a fiancée. As I want you people to learn something from my experiences, here is a bit of advice. And, kids, I particularly want you to pay attention to this: Don't get engaged to someone you've known only three weeks!

Naturally, my family was thrilled when I told them. "Pa," my mother said, "Terry's getting married again. Don't forget to milk the cows."

As much as JoJo and I loved each other, the media loved us more. *People* magazine wrote about us. The truth is I don't know whether or not I was really in love with her because I was never with her. We spent hours talking to each other on the phone. When we were apart we would read Scriptures together every morning. As she told a reporter, "Christianity is the center of our relationship, greater and higher than my ego and his ego."

I agreed. "That and heavy petting," I said.

People that claim opposites attract are probably right—but you notice they never tell you what happens after that? JoJo and I were both from the South; I was from Louisiana and she was from Southern California. She loved the city, I loved the country. She loved ballet, I loved square dancing. On her free nights she would fly to New York to see a Broadway show; I liked to go out into the pasture and watch my livestock. She liked neither country nor western. We agreed that after we were married we'd live in Pittsburgh during the season and on my farm the rest of the year. We were definitely opposites, maybe that's why there was such a strong attraction. Melissa Babich and I had had a small wedding and that hadn't worked. This time I wanted to start off right, this time I was definitely intending to stay married for the rest of my life. I believed I was really in love with her. I wanted a big wedding. I mean, my friends, a big wedding. I wanted to impress the caterers! So we planned to get married in Beverly Hills and invited hundreds of people.

A few weeks before the wedding JoJo was supposed to fly to Pittsburgh from New York after seeing *A Chorus Line*. Instead she called to tell me that not only wasn't she coming to Pittsburgh, but she didn't think we should get married.

That must have been some show. What she was really trying to tell me was that she didn't think she could give up her lifestyle and live on a ranch. Instead, what I heard was that she really didn't love me. And rather than accept that, I only wanted her more: She didn't love me? I'll win her love.

People get married for so many different reasons: love, desire, common values, a need for companionship, timing, luck. To make someone love you is probably the worst reason. No one can accurately predict why some marriages work so well, like my parents'. If I ever learn that secret I promise you I'm going to write a book about it.

But this is not that book. This is the other book, the book about marriages that fail and how to deal with the pain and sense of failure. With a few jokes thrown in.

JoJo and I had a beautiful wedding and lived happily ever after. Hey, there's one of those jokes right there.

When I married JoJo I believed it was for the rest of our lives. I remember after the wedding ceremony putting my arm around my dad and telling him how happy I was. And I was too. I mean, I thought I was. Well, maybe I wasn't.

I consider myself a sensitive human being. For example, if the great James Brown, one of my partners on the Fox football show, is having a bad hair day, I will be respectful of his feelings. And conversely, if I'm having a bad scalp day, he'll do the same for me. But when I married JoJo I had all the sensitivity of a professional football player. As I explained to a reporter, "I just like to get in my boots and jeans and go out on the ranch and not answer to anyone, to feed the stock. I may not come in until dinnertime and she'll have to learn to adjust. I won't leave the place without telling her and I will share everything that happened during the day with her when I get back, but I don't like reins on me and I won't ask her advice on running the ranch."

There are always people willing to give you their recipe for a successful marriage. As far as recipes go for a successful marriage, this one would be burnt toast. Well, I did try to share everything that happened on the ranch with her— Honey, the pigs didn't eat their slop today! Maybe Holly,

Louisiana, wasn't quite as exciting as Broadway, New York, but we did have a stop light that was changing all the time.

The road we lived on was so desolate it didn't even have a name. It was just called the Holly Road. But after we won our first Super Bowl the town honored me by naming the road Bradshaw Road. Unfortunately, we'd beaten the Dallas Cowboys in that game and northern Louisiana is heavily, heavily Cowboys territory. On Saturday nights Cowboys fans celebrated by shooting holes in my street sign. Bradshaw Road, huh? Bam! Bam! I'll give you dang Bradshaw Road. The town of Holly didn't have enough money in the budget to keep replacing the sign. That sign was shot to pieces, and every time a new one went up, it got shot up. JoJo just didn't seem to fit in there. I don't think she even had her own six-shooter.

Things went very well in our relationship for—maybe six weeks. Then she returned to her mother's home in Los Angeles. I flew out there and begged her to come back. She came back, then she left again. She joined another ice show and was back on the road again. We almost never spent more than a few days together at a time. I went to get her again. In the four years of marriage I think the longest time we actually spent together was six weeks.

Once again I was devastated. On the field I was the quarterback of one of the greatest football teams in history. We were winning Super Bowls. Off the field I was appearing in movies with Burt Reynolds, then the number one box office star in the world. I was recording country music albums. I was being offered my own TV series. I was the spokesman for a toupee company. Professionally my life was going very well. People must have thought, oh, that Terry, he's got some great life going. I didn't let anybody know how unhappy I was, I just kept smiling.

Inside I was dying. I felt like my life had turned into the makings for a great country album.

Finally, one day JoJo was just gone. That's the best way I can describe our entire relationship: She was just gone. Our marriage wasn't over, just our relationship. On occasion we would get together for a few days. She joined me for Super Bowl X, for example. When we were together it seemed nice to me.

I was in a quarterback meeting with Chuck Noll one afternoon when the sheriff showed up and handed me the divorce papers. Truly I was surprised. Just because we weren't living together, just because we were barely speaking, was that really a good reason to get divorced? Now imagine that you're in the middle of an important meeting, or in the middle of a major sale, or driving cross-country with a truckload of fresh fruit and you get served with divorce papers. Just exactly what do you do?

Ladies and gentlemen, that fruit must get delivered. You have got to make that sale. That is one important meeting. The Steelers fans did not care at all about my personal problems. Just imagine reading on the sports pages, "Bradshaw Going to Miss Three Games with Broken Heart!" My friends, that was not going to happen. I guarantee you that every time you watch a sports event some of those players are suffering from personal problems. Guaranteed. Their wives left them. Their money's gone. Well, that's basically the same thing, but you know what I mean. But you don't care about those players' problems at all, do you? Not because you're heartless—

you're a fine human being or you wouldn't be reading this book—but you have your own problems. I had a job to do and I had to learn how to do my job when my world was collapsing. I had to learn how to focus on my immediate problems. Practice. The game. I found during that time that the harder I worked the better I felt. In fact, statistically, the best year of my entire career was personally one of the most painful years of my life.

Whenever there has been a crisis in my life I've managed not to let it interfere with my professional life. The year I suffered through Divorce III was the year I won an Emmy for my work on Fox. I think I focused intently on my work because it temporarily relieved the pain.

I was making about $200,000 annually when JoJo filed for divorce. She asked for $1,000,000. We offered substantially less. While we were fighting over alimony I was still trying to win her back. Everybody reading this book who has loved someone who didn't love them back just keep breathing.

I guess that covers it. It happens to everybody. This is the place in the heart that country music comes from. If my life was a song it would have been titled something like *A Fool in Love*, or *I Tried to Give You My Heart but You Wanted My Most Recent IRS Return*. Her attorneys claimed I was hiding money. That just wasn't true. The amazing thing was that I still wanted to get back together with her.

One time she met me at a hotel and I gave her a pair of diamond earrings. Next thing I knew her attorney claimed that gift was proof we were back together, which meant she was entitled to more money I didn't have.

Finally she called and asked to come back to the ranch to

be with me. Men, that is the phone call all of us have waited for. Hallelujah! The woman we love who has rejected us has seen the error of her ways! Thank you, Lord, thank you! Naturally I tried to say no to her; I had been hurt so much I didn't want to risk it again, but she flew down to Lousiana and I picked her up at the airport. With roses.

We went out for dinner that night. I spent the next day working cattle while she stayed in the house. The situation was too uncomfortable for both of us. My heart had been hurt so bad I just couldn't open up to her. That's when I knew it was really over. I drove her to the airport.

When we went back to court I found out that while I was out in the field she was making lists of every item in my house. Furniture, candle holders, the buttons on my suit. She drew diagrams, she had page after page of my possessions.

Eventually her attorney had to compromise: He had to settle for the Mercedes with his fee rather than the Rolls.

CHAPTER 5

My Biggest Break—And How I Survived It

I BELIEVE IT IS PRETTY ACCURATE TO CLAIM THAT you're leading a harder life than absolutely necessary when you need to start identifying your marriages by Roman numerals. Marriage I to Melissa Babich was basically my starter marriage. Marriage II to JoJo was basic training camp. Marriage III to Charla Hopkins was definitely prime time. Definitely.

People tell you that if you fall off a horse the very best thing you can do is climb right back up on that horse and ride him again. But notice that they don't tell you what to do if you fall off again? Seems to me that falling off the same horse twice would qualify as pretty good evidence that you shouldn't be riding that horse in the first place. That horse has made its point.

That's pretty much the way I felt about marriage after my second divorce. I suspect at one time in their lives most men experience the same feelings I did: Either there was something wrong with me or there was something wrong with all the women in the world.

The only thing I couldn't figure out is how it got to all of them?

Everybody wants the same thing, a perfect relationship. We all want to be with somebody who just loves us all up, never does anything to irritate us, and enjoys the same things we do. And we all pretty much believe that is possible. Now, I want everyone who has had a perfect relationship to stand up right now, right where you are, and scream out just as loud as you can, "I have a perfect relationship! I have a perfect relationship!"

And don't you worry about people looking at you like you're crazy. Because if you try to tell anybody that you have a perfect relationship they already know you're crazy. There just isn't any such thing. The only real problem about being in a relationship is that it involves another person who isn't you. A person who has their own needs and desires. A person who just may not like cows or Gary Cooper movies.

But like everybody else I wanted to find the perfect relationship. I knew she had to be out there. Meeting women has never been easy for me. I have never considered myself good looking. Basically, I had grown up running past mirrors. Even when I had a mop of blond hair. I hadn't grown up believing that I was desirable to women. In fact, there were times I thought my name must be "Terry but," because a lot of women told me, "I really like you Terry, but . . ."

That changed when I became famous. I was the quarterback of the greatest football team in history. Just like the supermodels my picture was on the cover of *Sports Illustrated*—but I was wearing a helmet. But in that helmet I looked better than ever before. Fame made me attractive. All of a sudden my nose wasn't just broken and crooked, it was "heroic." My head wasn't bald, it was "dynamic," it "made a statement." Well sure it made a statement; it said, this boy's got no hair! But fame had made me attractive.

I did meet a lot of nice women, but none of them seemed to be right for me. I was beginning to accept the fact that some people are just meant to be single, that for whatever complicated reason they are not able to form strong emotional relationships, that they build walls that make it difficult for other people to get close to them, that they manage to be content with the simple things in life and while—

Then I met Charla Hopkins and I forgot all about that psychological stuff. I was at a party at a cowboy bar in Denver in 1982 when I looked up and saw her dancing. I remember she was wearing Wrangler's and a Western shirt. She looked like she'd been buttered into those jeans. I couldn't take my eyes off her. Eventually I just cut in on her partner and started dancing with her.

She was living in Houston, studying at the University of Houston. Charla was considerably younger than me. We dated for almost five years. Things were so nice between us that I didn't want to ruin it by getting married. Meanwhile she graduated and got her master's degree in marriage and family counseling. Maybe that should have been a message; if you get married again you're definitively going to need counseling.

I just didn't want to get married. I definitely did not want to get married. Let me make this really clear: No way did I want to get married. No *habla* marriage. We broke up and I didn't see her for several months. I was fine about it. Believe me, I was fine. When I finally called her just to say hello she told me sweet and nice, "Terry, I'm seeing somebody and it's time for us to go our separate ways. You're a sweet guy, but

I'm dating a lawyer here. And I can't talk to you now because we're getting ready to go to California and . . ."

I wanted to get married. I definitely wanted to get married. How could she do that to me? To me? Starting right at that very moment, far as I was concerned I had always wanted to marry her. The thought of losing her to . . . to a lawyer was just too much for me.

Now pay attention: I know most people think that the only reason I suddenly wanted to marry her was because she rejected me. And if you are one of those people, well, you are absolutely correct. I can't deny it. As I later came to understand through counseling, I couldn't bear the fact that she was able to break up with me on her terms. That's why I fought so hard to win her love—so I could break up with her on my terms. How sad is that? That's hard to admit, but that's exactly what I did. As long as a woman didn't want to be with me, I needed to be with her to prove that I was worth being with. But as soon as she wanted to be with me I could break up with her. The best way to win me was to reject me. Now, had I been a mature young man I would not have done something like that, and then I wouldn't have needed counseling, and then Dr. Bush would not have been able to afford that beautiful third child.

My ego just wouldn't allow me to accept the fact that some people—women, for example—didn't necessarily want to be with me. My response to rejection of any type has always been to work harder, to keep trying until I succeed. Especially when I wanted something. I wanted to be with Charla because she no longer wanted to be with me. And that is a sad fact. I respected her deeply for that. She certainly had grown in my estimation. Remember that lesson number two: Don't take actions just to make yourself feel better. Feeling bad is temporary. Eventually that feeling will go away. But a wife insists on staying forever.

I pursued her. I did everything she asked. I went to counseling. After hearing my story the counselor told me, "You do not need to marry this woman, Terry. This is not the woman for you. You have nothing in common. She may really be a nice person, but she's not the right person for you. Terry, this is not the woman for you. It's a big mistake." After considering that advice I took a very important step—I found another counselor.

As I have learned, the fact that I wanted to marry her didn't really have that much to do with her. It was about me. It was about all my own insecurities and fears, it was about my ego, about my competitive nature. I wanted to win. Although maybe it had a little bit to do with the way she looked in those jeans. And boy, did she look good in those jeans.

Finally, she agreed to marry me. To be my wedded wife. I was so relieved. I felt so good. I finally had what I wanted—so naturally I didn't want it anymore. Can you just imagine what it felt like to have fought as hard as possible to win the love of a beautiful woman, to fight through swamps and jungles, to battle fire-breathing dragons and swim through quicksand in the name of love? To meet your beloved's parents and buy a big ring? To invite hundreds of people and make the real commitment—hire a caterer? And then be sitting there just a few minutes before the wedding ceremony and suddenly realize: You know what? Maybe this isn't such a good idea.

That was my marriage. I knew it was a mistake for me, but I figured what's the worst that can happen?

A lot of smart people with advanced psychology degrees have earned their fortunes answering that question on an hourly basis.

We got married at the Little Chapel in the Woods at Texas Women's University. For a time I thought I was happy. After fourteen years of living and working in Pittsburgh, in the big city, the one thing I had been looking forward to was to finally live on my beloved four-hundred-acre ranch in Grand Cane, Louisiana, be around all my friends, and get involved in the weekly golf game. After living for so long away from home all I wanted to do was wake up to the chickens crowing on my ranch out in the middle of the country, go fishing, play with my dogs, work my cattle, show my horses, and go to bed to the hoot owls.

So I married a woman who wanted to go to law school and live near her own family. I wanted to make her happy so we moved to an apartment in Irving, Texas. Irving, Texas. That apartment was no more than five minutes away from Texas Stadium, the home of the Dallas Cowboys. Oh, my goodness gracious. I didn't move into the heart of Cowboy country, I moved right into the left ventricle of Cowboy country. I was surrounded by Cowboy fans, just surrounded by them—including my wife by the way—who continually reminded me in subtle ways that the Steelers had beaten the Cowboys in two Super Bowls. Subtle ways being things like people shouting at me—least they were shouting, not shooting—"Bradshaw, you $#^%%$# of $$#@!"

After winning those Super Bowls I had actually believed we had gotten the better of the Cowboys. Turns out I was just being set up for this move.

I moved to Texas to prove to her that she was more important to me than those things that really were most important to me. Now, I know I am not the only man to give up things of importance for the woman he thought he loved, but I do know how it turns out.

I have spent my whole entire life fighting to gain control of my life. I need to feel like I'm in charge. Have I mentioned that I called my own plays with the Steelers? I guess I was one of the last quarterbacks to really run my own game. That was important to me. Now the quarterbacks have sophisticated communications systems in their helmets: "Hey, Carlisle, how you doin', Sugar? You okay? Feeling good? That's nice. I got a real nice play for you here. Just stare down the strong safety, that's number forty-three—that's a four and a three written real close together. If he moves to his left, that's away from your throwing arm . . ."

I couldn't do that. I needed to call my own plays, I needed to be in control. Chuck Noll's way of controlling me was allowing me to be in control.

During my last seasons in Pittsburgh Chuck Noll was rebuilding the team. For a decade we had been a power team. My job was to hand the ball to Franco Harris or Rocky Bleier and get out of their way, then occasionally break up the rhythm with passes to Lynn Swann or John Stallworth. We weren't fancy, we were tough and we played strong fundamental football. But several of our great players were retiring or their skills had diminished. Adapting to that new reality Chuck basically installed a new offense. I had to change to succeed. That was hard for me to do. It required me to move away from my strengths. Maybe I looked like the same quarterback.

There's old Terry, how you doing there, buddy, but I never felt comfortable. Our playbook had changed considerably. Most of the time I was still calling my own plays, but I was getting them from a different playbook.

Too often that's what I felt like during all of my marriages. It may have appeared that I was calling the plays—I may have even thought I was calling the plays—but they all came from a little voice in my head. And I wasn't wearing any helmet. I was making myself unhappy trying to make other people happy. Admitting this is so difficult for me to do, but it is the truth. And it's a mistake a lot of people make. We form relationships to satisfy our needs, to feel good for a while. We don't even think about the needs of the other person. How sad is that? How embarrassing. It wasn't any of my wives' fault that I married them. They were all three nice people, pretty much innocent bystanders.

My third marriage wasn't like my first marriage where I wasn't in love with my wife. It wasn't like my second marriage where my wife wasn't in love with me. This was a whole different set of love problems. For a long time we got along fine. We were both so busy that we didn't have time to be unhappy. It seemed like I was constantly traveling somewhere to broadcast a football game or make a speech, appear in a commercial or do a TV show. Charla was always supportive of my career; in fact, she even took the initiative in helping me establish my speaking career. A lot of wives would have complained about how much time I had to spend on the road. But Charla loved me so much that she didn't seem to mind too much when I was gone.

I supported her through law school because I have always

believed people need to pursue whatever is in their heart. She really wanted to be a lawyer. It seemed like she was studying all the time. I didn't like it. I resented it. Truthfully, I was jealous. It seemed to me that being a lawyer was more important than being with me. Maybe selfishly, I wanted her to be with me when I was home. And deep inside I wanted her to complain when I wasn't home enough. I wanted her to tell me how much she and the kids missed me when I was gone. Instead, she was always supportive of me. Bye, Terry, love ya, have a good trip, see you Monday.

I need to feel loved. I don't mean just loved, I mean—all capital letters screaming from the top of the insurance company building for everybody to hear—loved. I need to be smothered in love. I need to feel that I am worth loving. That is the basic human need—and it is a need you can satisfy. The most worthwhile thing you can do today is tell someone that you love them. Now obviously I don't mean go up to someone in the street and tell them that you love them—you can get in real trouble for telling that to people.

I do mean make a point of telling it to the most important person or people in your life. Today. And if they're near you go ahead and hug on 'em. Hugs are cheap enough to give away as many as you can, and they make great gifts. In Marriage III I definitely suffered from I-love-you deprivation. We had some wonderful moments, but it was not a good marriage. And as time went on it deteriorated. I'd find myself sitting in a hotel room being absolutely miserable and not having the slightest idea what to do about it.

I still have a hard time believing that it is so difficult to be married to me. I mean, I think I'd be great to be married to—I like golf and fishing, spending time with horses, being in the country, and loving your family. I'd be perfect for me. But after many hours of therapy I have finally become convinced of one thing: In each of my marriages I married the wrong person. When I'm not happy I can be erratic and unpredictable. I'm moody and sometimes not as nice as I mean to be. Let me make one thing very clear: I bear the responsibility for the deterioration of our marriage. Charla and I had some fine years together and together we produced two beautiful young women.

But our needs were very different. I had to do the best acting job of my life to convince myself I was happy, but truthfully I was one miserable human being. I just wasn't leading my own life.

We both knew it wasn't working. At one point Charla suggested we go to marriage counseling. I sat there listening to the counselor talk about sharing and being sensitive to each other's needs and I didn't say anything and I didn't learn anything because I was angry. Once again I had married the wrong person for me. Probably not for somebody else, but for me. I was angry because I was angry and I didn't know why I was angry. I was angry because we didn't seem to have much in common: She wanted to be a lawyer, and I wanted to go fishing. She wanted to study, and I wanted to go look at the horses. I was just angry and sad and I didn't know what to do about it.

I know for sure the three best words in the English language are "I love you." But I can also tell you the worst words. One afternoon Charla walked into my office and said them. "We need to talk." My friends, nothing good has ever followed those words.

It sure didn't in this case. This was that inevitable day that neither one of us ever wanted to come. She told me, "I just don't love you anymore."

I was devastated. Totally ripped apart. It seemed like all the blood drained right out of my body. I couldn't see her and she was standing no more than three feet away from me. That statement could not have been any more clear, but I had to ask anyway, "What do you mean?"

"I just don't have any feelings for you. You're a good man, but I just don't have any feelings for you."

I panicked. This was the worst fear of my life coming true: The woman I didn't love didn't love me. But as soon as she said those words out loud I wanted her back more than ever. Isn't human nature wonderful? You stop loving somebody right up until the time they stop loving you. And then you realize that you have loved them forever. And you have to win them back. You have to make them love you again so you can stop loving them again. Which is what I tried to do; I did all the things that we all do in those situations, which basically can be summed up as, I made a fool of myself. I begged, I pleaded, I said I'm sorry. I cried. I did some really crazy things to try to win her back.

Yes, people did notice the difference between those things and my normal crazy things.

When you are in the middle of a situation like this you really do believe no one has ever felt as much emotional pain as you're feeling. You don't care if the sun comes up the next morning. You feel so alone, so completely worthless. You feel like it would be impossible to ever feel as bad as this ever again. I know this is true because I've felt that way several times.

When you feel that way it's important to understand that you are not alone. There may not be a lot of real good advice I can offer, but I can definitely tell you that you are not alone. More than that, I can promise you that eventually you'll heal. I said, you will heal!

In this situation I definitely wanted to reconcile with her and work things out so we could spend the rest of our lives together. Either that or I definitely never wanted to see her again as long as we lived.

Think it's easy being me? I knew that there was only one thing I really wanted—and what that one thing was depended pretty much on the time or the day or my mood.

At one point when we were trying to work things out Charla told me she needed her space. So I moved into a nice apartment upstairs in the horse barn, which was about a football field away from the main house. One thing I guarantee, if a woman ever again tells me she needs her space, I will give her all the space she could possibly want—it's just that I won't be in it. I lived in that apartment for a little over a year, hoping desperately the whole time that one day I'd get that phone call from her telling me she was willing to try again.

This is where we get back to dealing with adversity. This was as tough a time as I had ever struggled through in my life. In public I had to do my job, which was being Terry Bradshaw. I had to smile and laugh, I had to talk football, I had to give meaningful speeches. I knew that nobody really cared what was going on in my personal life, that wasn't their concern: Ah, Terry, sorry to hear you're living out there in a barn, but whattya think, can the Giants really beat the Bears?

I was fortunate that I had my work, which kept me busy, to

distract me. I would forget about the situation at home for hours at a time, even a full day. Almost everybody who has lost another person they really cared about knows this feeling. It's like in the cartoons when they shoot a hole through Sylvester the Cat and he walks around with a big round hole in his stomach that you can see right through. That empty feeling never goes away. Within a few hours my emotions would range from "We've won the Super Bowl" to "How do you do—the IRS has assigned your case to me."

Meanwhile I was giving the most powerful speeches of my life. Some people wear their heart on their sleeve, my guts were hanging out. I talked mostly about relationships and family. And I felt it, oh, Lord I felt it.

And often when I spoke I would break down in tears on the stage. I could just imagine what people were saying: "That was some powerful speech. That boy made hisself cry. He must be really feelin' that, 'cause I've seen him act and he can't act that good!"

When I was away from the ranch, people would be so nice to me; generally people have always been nice to me, and I would begin to feel good about myself. Maybe I'm not such a jerk. Maybe after all I'm a decent person who made a mistake. And then I would get home and that empty feeling would return.

I couldn't eat, I didn't sleep. I suffered. Fortunately I didn't have any hair to fall out. I was as unhappy as I have ever been in my life. I talked to everybody I knew about it until I was as bored hearing about it as they were. When I was in Los Angeles to do the Fox show my friend Jeff Quinn and I would always try to run four miles. We'd start running and I'd start talking about my problems and how badly I hurt and how depressed I was and before I knew it we'd run six miles, seven miles and I was still talking. "Gee, Jeff," I asked, "why didn't you say something?"

"Uggghhh," he gasped. "Ugghhhhhhh."

I was so deeply depressed the doctors had to put me on drugs to deal with it. At times I couldn't breathe. One time in L.A. I thought I was dying. I laid down on the couch and couldn't get up. Jeff Quinn got a doctor who realized I was having a severe anxiety attack. I tried everything to understand what was wrong with me. I read psychology books, I read self-help books, and then I started reading my Bible.

Pretty interesting book.

I started working on me. I started seeing a counselor, Bill Bush. I accepted responsibility for my own actions. I am, I began to understand, a product of my environment. If you've grown up in an environment in which your family gets together every weekend, as I did, then that's how you want to live your life.

I grew up watching my mother wait on my dad hand and foot. My dad would come home from work every day and sit down in his chair and smoke his pipe and read and watch television and go to bed. My mother took care of him and their three sons. Only once in my entire life did I see my dad raise his voice to my mother. That's how I was raised. That's what I knew and at times it was tough for me to square that with all the changes in society. From the time I grew up marriage and family relationships have come all the way from the Ozzie Nelsons to the Ozzy Osbornes.

Now just hold on, I don't believe that a woman needs to be

100 percent submissive and that the man's job is to accept that. I understand that each person has to pursue his or her own goals to be happy, and happy people make stronger relationships. But my concept of what a marriage should be was based on my parents' relationship.

Finally, after about a year living in the barn—I describe it as living on death row—I realized I just couldn't go on like that any longer. It was just too painful for me. Charla and I decided it was time to go our separate ways.

I suspect some people think that success, money, fame, and four Super Bowl championships—in which I called my own plays—somehow protect you from the same emotional pain that most everyone experiences. I can tell you right on this page, and it's printed in ink so it won't fade away, that that is not true.

During this period I turned for emotional survival to those things in my life that I knew best: my faith, my work, and my friends. I just got up every day and did what needed to be done. Talking to friends made me realize that just about everybody has suffered through loss—and got through it and over it. At times I just wanted to pull the covers over my head and stay there—for two or three years. But obviously I couldn't. Imagine how the Fox show would look with James Brown, Howie Long, and Terry Under the Blanket. I forced myself to lead my life.

I got hit very hard during my career. One time Turkey Jones turned me upside-the-ground and drilled for oil. Another time Dick Butkus hit me so hard I couldn't focus; our trainer came running out and held up some fingers. "Terry," he said urgently, "how many fingers am I holding up?"

I shook my head. "Come on, Tony," I said, "you know I've never been very good in math."

My point is that eventually the pain went away. Some of the injuries I suffered affected me permanently; I'll never run the Olympic marathon for example, but the pain went away. Just as my divorces have affected me permanently—but I knew that someday the emotional pain would also go away. And it did.

I have been through three divorces. I want to make it real clear that these divorces were my fault. The women I married were fine people whose main fault was me. I'm mad at myself for causing them pain. And I'm embarrassed by my own failures. And disappointed, very disappointed.

Divorce is so painful. Now, people, like me you may have children, and someday those little children may come to you with that innocent look in their eyes and ask you, "Mom" (or Dad), "what's the definition of insincere?" When that happens you just tell them that insincere is what a divorce lawyer is when he tells you, "I'm sorry to hear about your divorce, Mr. Bradshaw."

With all the different kinds of insurance it's possible to buy today have you ever wondered why insurance companies don't sell "divorce insurance"? I'll tell you why. Because they want to make a profit, that's why! More than half the adults in this country have gone through at least one divorce—of course thanks to me there are two couples out there who can stay together without messing up that statistic. I don't this know for certain, but I have been told that there are more divorces in this country every year than there are Mercedes-Benzes sold. Now think about that; more people would rather have a divorce than a great automobile. More than that, a divorce usually costs more and it doesn't even come with bucket seats and a roadside assistance warranty.

I never want to go through that pain again. In football, if after three tries you end up in pretty much the same place you started, you punt. You just got to admit that you are not moving forward and give up the ball. Three and out. And when you get the ball back again, if you're smart and you're calling your own plays—which I did, by the way—you try a different strategy. You recognize that the old plays don't work.

But too often in life we just keep running the same plays. After three tries at marriage I was pretty much back where I'd started, although I was substantially poorer for the experiences. It was obvious to me that the only way I could prevent the same thing from happening again was to change my strategy. I had to figure out what was wrong with me. That's when I began to figure out that I had been choosing the wrong people. No matter how good they looked in jeans.

I need a woman who shares my values, who enjoys the same or similar things that I enjoy, and knows what matters to her. And as long as I'm ordering, I definitely would like her to fit comfortably into jeans. I do believe that someday I'll meet that person. I'm a hopeless romantic. I may be the number-one fan of the American Movie Classics channel. And I just don't believe He would have put me through all this without a reason, without a plan for a big finish. Someone I'll be real happy to come home to.

I am an optimist. Once there was a man who dressed in a purple court jester's outfit and rode around on his bicycle collecting horse manure in a burlap sack. Later I found out that he needed that fertilizer for an organic garden he had planted. Well, one spring I saw him riding on his bicycle—followed by a woman dressed in a purple court jester's outfit, riding on her bicycle with a burlap sack thrown over her shoulder. So I figure if a guy who rides around on his bicycle dressed in a purple court jester's outfit collecting manure in a burlap sack could find a woman who also rode around on a bicycle in a purple outfit collecting manure, there definitely is someone for everyone.

There are lessons to be learned. I believe I am a much better man now than I ever was while I was married. I'm still not perfect. For example, I still smoke cigars inside my house. I curse when it seems to be necessary. But when I needed my faith to help me get through all this I found it once again, and it made all the difference. Now I read my Bible regularly. I go to church often. I try to be more careful in the way I treat other people. And as much as I valued my family and friends before, I feel that so much more strongly now.

I could tell you what I've learned but it wouldn't do much good. I can't help anyone in matters of the heart. People wounded by love feel that no one else has ever been hurt so bad, that no one else could truly appreciate the depth of their loss. And that's probably true too—in every single situation. Each heart has a mind of its own. I wouldn't dare claim when it comes to someone else's emotional pain that I've been there, 'cause I haven't. My situations are mine, you'll have to suffer your own pain. I'd be happy to let you cry on my shoulder, but you have to experience it for yourself.

The fact is that during the barn year not one person whose shoulder I cried on was able to help me get through the pain.

They tried, but I couldn't hear them. I knew they just couldn't understand. So I can't help anyone else. We each have to wallow in our own slop. One thing that is worth mentioning though, is that the very worst day of my suffering was the first day of my getting beyond it. And for those people who have lost someone they love and think they will never recover from that loss, I am here on this page to tell you that is not true. Time passes, memories lose their sharp edges, new jeans appear.

Getting over an intense relationship is probably the most difficult thing I've ever done in my life. Normally I don't waste a lot of brain cells thinking about yesterday, but moving a person out of my mind is a long hard process.

I survived to be ready to love again. I am a happy man. I have my renewed faith. I'm thinking about getting myself a bicycle and a burlap bag. Hey, you never know.

Because I have never stopped believing in the possibility of true love.

CHAPTER 6

KEEPING THE FAITH

ONE AFTERNOON I WAS ON A FLIGHT LEAVING DALLAS HEADED FOR San Francisco, where I was scheduled to make a corporate speech. The plane raced down the runway, the nose wheel lifted off and—boom! The pilot slammed it back down on the runway and hit the brakes. No big deal, I thought, just a minor problem, no way the captain would try to take off if there was something seriously wrong with the airplane. However, I did notice a bead of sweat forming on my forehead.

The pilot never said a word. He taxied back to the end of the runway, got back in line for takeoff and about ten minutes later the plane was barreling down the runway, the nose wheel lifted off the ground and—wham! That plane slammed back down on the runway.

Now the pilot had my attention. "There's just a little problem," he finally explained, "just a little light that keeps coming on. I'm gonna take it back to the gate where they'll fix it and we can get going again. I'm positive it's just a loose bulb and I'd sure appreciate everyone just staying in your seats."

Naturally I was my usual cool and calm. When the flight attendant opened that front door I was gone. I mean, I was history. Wow, what was that blur? That weren't no blur, that was Terry Bradshaw getting off the plane. 'Course I had to move fast, an entire planeload of passengers was right on my heels.

The pilot tried to head me off. He tried to convince me to get back on the plane—but first he had to wait while I hyperventilated. Finally I got my breath back and explained very calmly that the only way I was getting back on that plane was if he drove it on the interstate to San Francisco.

By necessity, I spend a lot of my life on airplanes. Flying had never much bothered me until my kids were born, then all of a sudden my life took on new meaning. I wanted to be around to watch them grow up. So for about two years I was terrified every time I had to get on an airplane. There were times when I was so scared before a flight I'd sit in my car in the airport parking lot and cry. In flight the slightest turbulence would terrify me; my head would go down between my legs. It was embarrassing.

I finally got control of it. Fortunately, I had some help. I remembered to rely on my faith. I realized that there was nothing I could do about my fears. But I was comfortable with my salvation.

There isn't a day in my life that goes by that I don't spend at least a few minutes focusing on my faith. I mean, really thinking about it. My faith brings into my life a place to find calm. Now don't worry, I'm not going to get all evangelical. May I have an amen on that, brothers and sisters. But I know that for me it's necessary to have a refuge to visit. Other people may not find it in religion. They may find the same peace that I find in other places. Just finding it is what matters.

My relationship with the Lord has endured from my childhood—although admittedly at times I haven't been quite as good a Christian as I wanted to be. I was brought up a God-fearing Baptist. And I was taught that the Lord is mighty, yes He is, and that He moves in mysterious ways. Amen to that, brother, amen to that. And that He is watching us, oh, my brothers and sisters. He is always watching us. And He knows, I said He knows, when we have been faithful. Because He knows what we are thinking.

That part about Him knowing what we are thinking gave me real trouble growing up. I tried to be a good Christian, I went to church, read my Bible, I even gave testimony at other churches. And when I did speak at those churches I told those people that I had been faced with sin and I had given it up. Which technically wasn't exactly true.

I knew what sin was. Sin was what I was thinking when I was out on a date. But I hadn't actually given up sin. I hadn't had the opportunity to make that choice. In fact, to be completely truthful, when I was a teenager I faced my first real paradox: Occasionally when I was on a date I found myself praying I would have the opportunity to see what sin looked like. In the flesh.

But I believed. Oh, I definitely believed. While I was at Louisiana Tech I spent one summer working as a youth minister for a local Methodist church. I wasn't very good at it. First of all, I wasn't even Methodist. I was a God-fearing, Hell-raising, shout it out loud brothers and sisters, Praise the Lord Baptist. I was not a polite, let us now pray, Methodist. I don't remember what I told those kids. Probably don't drink alcohol. Treat your parents with respect. Don't do anything on dates that I can't get away with.

I was definitely not qualified for that job. I grew up believing that God always had his hand on me, although I didn't quite know why He had picked me. But I just always felt different as a child. Those of you who understand what I mean about feeling different—which is probably pretty much everyone—know that feeling. I looked at things differently from most kids. I acted differently. I didn't join crowds. I didn't hang out with the other kids. I was pretty much a loner. Basically, I was a nerd. I didn't care, in fact I didn't even know it. But I always felt the presence of God, this spirit; I was always in tune with that. I never said much about it because I didn't want the other kids to think I was weird. I didn't want them laughing at me.

What He gave me was a passion for the game of football and the talent to play it. I believed that He put me here to throw a football. That was my blessing. I didn't exactly understand how football fit into His grand plan, I just accepted it. Football was the one thing in my life that fulfilled me. It was just about the only time I felt completely comfortable being me. And because I believed that He had this plan for me I could accept sitting on the bench in high school and college, waiting for the rest of the plan to be revealed.

Maybe that seems a little naïve, but the reality is that everything I have in my life I have because I believed that. I believed it without doubt. I had absolutely no evidence, but what I did have was my faith. When times got difficult, I had faith. I persevered.

Admittedly, I wasn't always consistent in my faith. Like most people when I was bad I called on it and when things were going well I forgot all about it. Less than perfect would probably be a good way of describing me. A lot less than perfect. I mean, believe me here, a whole lot less than perfect. I'd like every person reading this book who has never done anything wrong to raise your right hand. Raise it high.

I don't see any raised hands. Figuratively, I mean.

When I started my playing career most of the interviews I did were with the Christian media. I said all the right things. And I tried to be a good Christian, I truly did, but temptation blitzed me. Hit me harder than Butkus. I was a young man from Hall Summit in the big city. I definitely wasn't the role model I wanted to be. At first I was very disappointed in myself. Once, I remember, I got really furious at myself for throwing a stupid pass and started cursing myself out; then I got mad at myself for cursing, so I cursed myself for cursing. It was definitely confusing trying to figure out how I fit in the world.

I definitely did not fit in with the Pittsburgh Steelers. My rookie year would have made a great plot for a movie: A young, innocent man with a rocket throwing arm gets drafted by a pro football team stocked with grizzled veterans. This was still the old NFL, where games were played outdoors in the freezing cold on frozen turf, where players took such pride in their recklessness and toughness that they were embarrassed to still have their own teeth. In this movie the young, innocent man would take charge of the team and by the strength of his character not only lead them to victory, but convince them to embrace his Christian way of life.

That's not exactly the way it worked in real life. Once Andy Russell came to hear me speak to a church group. Oh, man, I got into it that day, I just let it fly. I was feeling it; I said, I was feelin' it! The most important organ in the human body is the tongue, and when I opened my mouth those words just flew out. They came out so fast there was a traffic jam at my teeth. It didn't matter, the words came directly from my heart. Andy sat there with his own mouth sort of flopped open. I think he was in shock. I'm sure he was thinking, this is our new quarterback? Uh oh. Successful NFL quarterbacks had traditionally been men like Bobby Layne, who was so tough he played without a face mask and "Broadway Joe" Namath, who was rarely seen without a beautiful woman and was so tough that he made panty hose commercials and nobody laughed. I spent my free time witnessing in church.

Faith doesn't play much of a role in professional football. I mean, no matter how hard I prayed, Dick Butkus was still going to show up to play on Sunday. I never prayed for success on the football field. Just imagine the pressure that would put on God. Suppose I prayed to complete a pass while the defensive back was praying just as righteously for an interception? What's a merciful God to do in that situation? If you accept Jesus as your Savior then you know He loves each person playing the game equally, and that He loves everybody in the stands. That's his job. I don't believe God singled me out for success; I don't think He really cares who wins the Super Bowl. He gave me the tools to succeed and the will, but the rest was really up to me.

It was years after I retired that players began thanking God for their success. I'm really uncomfortable with that. I remember, for example, interviewing Kurt Warner after the Rams had beaten Tampa to win the league championship and get into the Super Bowl. The first thing Kurt did was look up to heaven and say, "Thank you, Jesus!"

But yet when the Rams lost the Super Bowl I didn't hear any "Thank you, Jesus." That's the problem—and I don't mean to pick on Kurt Warner; it's just that he was the first player I thought of to make this point—this happens all the time. Too often it's "Thank you, Jesus" for the good, but what about thanking Jesus when bad things happen? If you're only acknowledging the presence of God when He does something good for you, what kind of message is that sending out? That He only rewards those who are successful? That's not what I believe.

I believe that all prayer is answered—but it just may not be the answer you're looking for. You may be praying, as I did: O God, O God, please, please save my marriage, bring us back together. But still the marriage ends. And you're upset, you think the Lord didn't answer your prayers. You forget that you didn't ask Him before you got married for His advice. You didn't ask for His help getting in, but you want His help getting out. Maybe wrong, maybe right. Hey, I'm still mad at Adam and Eve. If it hadn't been for them we'd be all right.

I don't expect to hear a player earnestly thanking God for letting his team lose anytime soon. So I think it probably would be better if players simply kept their relationship with the Lord private. I'm pretty certain God isn't watching the game on television, so it probably isn't necessary to broadcast your appreciation. If you feel it, He knows it.

I rarely asked Him in my prayers to fulfill my needs or desires. I can't honestly say I never asked, I might have slipped in one or two little suggestions. But I never prayed for victory. Why would I? There was nothing I could tell Him that I wanted that He didn't already know about. He knows the desires in my heart. He knows what I need. And I believe that if I'm faithful and obedient to His word He will bless me more than I can ever imagine.

There is a story told in church about a deeply religious woman whose home was flooded. This was a devoted Christian. She read her Bible every day. She could quote the Scriptures. In the morning when they opened the church doors she was there waiting. So as the bottom floor of her house filled up with water the police came to take her to safety. "Oh no," she told them, "God will provide for me."

The waters kept rising and she climbed to the second floor. A man came by in a rowboat and offered to take her to safety. "Oh no," she said again, "God will provide for me."

The waters just kept rising and finally she climbed out on the roof. A helicopter came and dropped a rope to her. "Oh no," she said, "God will provide for me."

Eventually the flood waters swept her off the roof and she drowned. Drowned dead. When she woke and found herself in heaven she was furious. I mean, this was one angry woman. She demanded to see God. When she came face-to-face with Him she said, "How could you do that to me? I went to church every day. I read my Bible cover to cover. I quoted the Scriptures. I gave to charity. I did everything you asked and you still let me drown. Why didn't you save me?"

"Save you?" God said, "What do you want from me? I sent you a policeman, a rowboat, and a helicopter."

I definitely believe in the power of prayer—but that doesn't stop me from taking action. Way back in 1971, for example, I was flying on a private plane with about two other men and three women. As we were preparing to land in Lubbock, Texas, the pilot told us we had a bit of a problem—the landing gear was jammed and wouldn't come down. A bit of a problem? If that's a bit of a problem I wanted to know what that man considered a sizeable problem. The women immediately started praying. The pilot told me what to do. I had to reach down and free the jammed wheels, then manually lower them into landing position. I didn't have time to pray. Finally I managed to get the wheels free and we landed safely.

I figured I had saved us. I was feeling pretty good about it, until one of the women told me, "Thank God, Terry. We were all praying so hard God would give you the strength to get the wheels down. And He did."

I believe that God gave me a brain and expects me to use it. If, for example, I get sick I'm not going to waste time wondering why God did that to me. I'm not going to pray that He cures me. And I'm definitely not going to lie in bed and die without a fight because He does instill in all of us the ability to fight and struggle. He gave mankind the ability to think, to create, and to solve problems. I'll go to the doctor. I'll take medicine. I'll do whatever I can to be cured. If He wants to heal me He will; if He doesn't want to then I'll just move on.

If I didn't fight I'd be like that woman in the flood. Why didn't you have your gall bladder out? Why didn't you have chemo? Why didn't you get a tetanus shot? That's why I put it there.

I pray for my children, I pray for my family and friends, I

pray for peace in the world, and I pray that the Lord will help me become a better person.

During my playing career I was active in Christian athlete groups, working with people like Roger Staubach. I even served on the board of Christian Athletes. In Pittsburgh, with another player—and I can't remember who it was so you just go ahead and make up somebody—we started holding chapel services before our games. Later on in my career we even had a team chaplain, who held a service before each practice.

But, for the first time in my life, I moved away from my faith. A lot of things happened that I wasn't prepared to deal with. I felt tremendously guilty about the failure of my first marriage—in my family marriage was a life sentence. Divorce was something you whispered about so the kids wouldn't hear. Added to that was my depression over losing my starting quarterback job. Playing football was the one thing in my life I knew I could do well, and I was doing poorly. I was sitting on the bench. The fans were booing me—they didn't even like the way I was sitting. And I was living in Pittsburgh, a nice city but I definitely was not a city person.

I was miserable. I was moody and depressed. I started drinking and hustling women. Worse, I enjoyed it. But the more I enjoyed it the more guilty I felt for enjoying it. That's when I met and married JoJo Starbuck. When we first met, I thought that was God's way of forgiving me for being such a jerk. Turned out He was actually punishing me. Our apartment was just full of religious books, but we were never there together long enough to read them.

I came back to the church during my third divorce. I hadn't been a bad person, I didn't do things to hurt people, but I wasn't content within myself. At the end of the year I spent living in the apartment in the barn my soon to be third ex-wife told me that she no longer loved me. That our marriage was over. If it's possible to identify the moment in your life when you hit bottom that was—ow! That wasn't just hitting bottom, that was smashing into it—on Father's Day, 1999. And let me tell you, that bottom is hard. Charla was really worried about me, so she called the preacher to come out to the house to talk to me. We sat talking on the porch for a time and finally he asked me, "Terry, are you saved?"

"Saved" meaning that I have accepted the Lord in my life? That I truly believe that He was the son of God? That he died on the cross and was resurrected three days later and ascended into heaven? I had been saved as a child by Brother Buchanan, but at that time I really didn't understand what that meant. It was just something people did. I certainly didn't feel any differently after I got saved. Maybe I was hoping He'd start giving me some extra help on tests in school, but being saved hadn't caused any changes in my life that I had noticed.

"No," I said.

"Would you like to be?"

What I wanted most was for the pain I was feeling to go away. "Yes," I said, "I would."

We went over to the barn and he started praying the sinner's prayer. In my life I had never experienced anything I couldn't explain. I'd never seen a ghost or an alien or had an out-of-body experience—although at times linebackers had attempted to separate the various parts of my body. There is nothing more alarming than being tackled by two defensive players and having each of them grab hold of a leg, then hearing one of them yell, "Make a wish." But something happened in that barn that day. As the pastor started praying I believe the Holy Spirit came over me. It was as if the demons were being flushed from my body. I started sweating. My whole body was shaking. That pastor's voice was booming in my head; it was so loud it was frightening. It was the most amazing experience of my life. Oh yeah, I was saved, brothers and sisters, I tell you right now, I was saved. Maybe I didn't exactly see the Lord, but I definitely felt His presence. He gang-tackled me all by Himself.

In the Baptist church it's traditional that after accepting Jesus as your Savior you have to get baptized. In front of the entire congregation they dunk your head in water and pull you back out. It signifies rebirth. So the following Sunday I went to church and was baptized. Afterward the preacher asked me if I wanted to speak to the congregation. Because I was well known the preacher felt my experience might have an impact on other people.

Charla was with me. She did not want me to speak. Take the Fifth, she said. Maybe not exactly that, but she did not want me to speak. I think she was a little concerned about what I might say. I know myself well enough to understand that fear. Hey, when I open my mouth anything is possible. I'm generally as interested as everyone else to hear what comes out.

I tried to express in words the joy I was feeling. For the first time in so long it just seemed like everything was going to be all right. When I get enthusiastic about something, I get real enthusiastic. I mean, I dive into the deep end. I mean, I climb the highest mountain. And this was no different. One time I needed a few office supplies, for example, so I went into a stationery superstore. I was overwhelmed. I just wanted to buy everything; I just kept throwing things in my basket. Colored pencils, markers, papers, folders, empty boxes. Now, I don't like to admit that I bought too much, but if anybody should need an electronic stapler I have a couple of . . . five or six . . . a dozen that I'm not using at the moment.

I had always acknowledged that I was a Christian, but until this time I had never really accepted it in my heart. This was a very different experience. I asked my younger brother Craig to take me down to a Christian bookstore so I could learn more about what had happened.

I spent $4,000 in that bookstore. I am not exaggerating—$4,000. Fortunately for me, though, that store didn't sell electronic staplers or it might have been much worse.

My life definitely changed that day. I still do a lot of things that make my little girls cringe. I still use foul language when it is appropriate. Like on a golf course. Drink. Date pretty ladies. But I also go to church when I can. I pray regularly. I read my Bible almost every day. I've read at least $4,000 worth of Christian books. I listen to gospel music; in fact I even recorded a gospel album with the great Jake Hess. We were looking for a catchy title so we came up with *Terry and Jake*. And my conscious thought process often centers on spiritual matters.

I found what I needed for me; not for anybody else, for me. It has made a difference in my life. But I do not proselytize. Do it? I can barely pronounce it. What it means is I don't try to convince anyone to adopt my faith. I have respect for all faiths. I don't know that much about them, but I respect them. I talk about my faith because it is an integral part of who I am, but I would never try to push it on anybody.

I certainly am not an evangelist—although sometimes I think it might be great fun. I watch these people on TV sometimes and when they get to yabba-dabba-dooing I just love it. I love it. It's something I can do, yes I can, brothers and sisters. I said, Yes! Yes, I can! Because God said you have to walk in faith. He didn't say you have to walk step-by-step. He didn't say you have to talk to the birds. He didn't say you have to move a tree or move a rock or get in your truck. You have to walk—Are you listening to me—I said, are you listening to me!

My friends, and you are my friends, I met a man the other day and this man said to me, "Brother Terry, I have been having trouble at home with my left eyeball. I haven't been able to see and I have terrible earaches. Would you lay your hands on me and give me the gift of God's healing power?" And I laid my hands upon that man. And I felt the power of the Lord surge through me. And it shook me to my very core, my friends, it shook me. And that man looked upon me with tears in his eyes. And he said, "I can see! I can see!" That man could see. Was it me? Was it him? Was it my faith—

I don't believe any of that. One thing I do know, though, if I really did have the power to heal, if I could heal people, I'd start with myself. I'd put hair on my head. Then I'd go on the road with Terry's Healing Seminar and make my fortune.

But that's not how my faith works, not in day-to-day life. My faith is personal. I'm not the kind of person who goes around blessing people; just imagine, "Bless you, Howie, for that insightful report on the Oakland Raiders." And I never,

ever judge people based on their religious beliefs; if people truly believe that holding on to a doorknob while singing *Louie Louie* makes them a better person—well, then it does. What I did was integrate my faith into my regular life rather than building my life around my faith. I didn't change my life, I tried to change the way I acted in my life. What my faith provides for me is a strong foundation on which I can live my life. It serves as a pretty good reference point for me to determine right and wrong, although it doesn't stop me from doing not perfectly right on occasion.

One of the things I've done is read the entire Bible. I'd read it before, in sections, never from the beginning to the end. It took me three years to read it cover to cover. It's basically a history lesson, except for all those begots. For a book with no sex in it, there definitely was a lot of begettin' going on in those days.

When I first read the Bible as a child I remember that I had a whole lot of questions. I wanted to believe everything I read. This was God's biography, it had to be true. But there were some things in there that definitely were a challenge to me. If Jonah really was swallowed by a whale, for example, how did he breath in there? If Moses really did separate the Red Sea, how could the Hebrews walk through all that mud that was left on the bottom? If Noah really did take two of every species on the ark for forty days and forty nights, who cleaned up after those animals? Hey, I used to get yelled at by my dad for sneaking the hunting dog in through my bedroom window and letting him sleep there. That was just one dog. I wondered with two of every animal onboard who cleaned up the ark? Whew, just imagine what that ark smelled like down below.

And I always wondered why Noah brought two mosquitoes with him. That was the last chance to get rid of them once and for all and he had to bring them with him. Why? What good are mosquitoes?

Eventually I figured out that it wasn't necessary to take those Bible stories literally.

The Bible might be the original "how to" book. Well, except of course, for how to beget. But basically it lays down some commonsense rules for leading a healthy life. It isn't a recipe book. It's doesn't give you every detail, you have to figure out a lot of things for yourself. It doesn't tell me, for example, how to ask a woman for a date. Or what part of my ranch the IRS will allow me to deduct. It doesn't even tell me the simple things like should I get cable or a satellite dish?

My faith fulfills me. It brings me peace. Even when I'm struggling, when I'm not on my best behavior, I don't beat myself up about it anymore. I'm a human being, I know I'm going to sin; I know I'm going to get short-tempered, I know I'm going to hurt people's feelings. I know I'm going to go through periods when I'm having way too many drinks, when I'm telling way too many bad jokes, when I'm not being the best person in the world.

And those are the times that I am particularly thankful for His mercy.

But when I am less than I'd like to be, at least now I'm aware of it. My faith has taught me what I'm supposed to be doing. I try to work on it. I try to be better.

I've never really been very public about my Christian beliefs. I'm not ashamed of my faith, or embarrassed by it. But I know preaching can sometimes make other people uncomfortable and I don't want to do that. So I don't so much speak it as much as I try to live it.

When I went on a promotional tour for my last book, the wonderfully funny, insightful, revealing *It's Only a Game,* I decided to try something I'd never done before. I tried getting up every morning and smiling. I mean really s-m-i-l-i-n-g. I mean a late-night-infomercial-real-estate-deal smile, which is something I had often preached but sometimes failed to practice. During this two-week trip I was determined to greet each day, and each person I met each day, with a big smile. I was going to be nice to everybody; no matter what happened I was determined to keep smiling.

The results were phenomenal. The reaction from people was phenomenal. When people got mad at me, when they were fussing and fuming I just smiled and tried to be as nice as I could. And it worked. People can't help but like you, they can't help responding to you positively when they feel friendship and joy coming from you. They can't help it.

I know I'm a work in progress. But I also know when I am totally content with myself, totally at peace—and that can last for days at a time or it might just be a few minutes in a whole week—it's when I believe I am living the Christian faith that I am supposed to be living.

One thing I learned playing football was that what worked for me did not necessarily work for anybody else. As a quarterback there were a lot of technical things I did wrong. I made my coaches so crazy that the Steelers had to open a special mental health clinic just for them—thankfully they were able to save most of those fine people. The rest I still visit from time to time at the place. The point is that my faith works for me. What I'm suggesting is that you find whatever it is in your life that makes you feel content, that makes you feel at ease with yourself, that permits you to forgive yourself when you need it. Maybe it's your faith, for some people it's meditation. It doesn't really matter what it is. What does matter is that you find it.

It really is simple; treat yourself with kindness, do the best you can and accept the fact that you are doing the best you can, and do onto others as you would have them do unto you.

CHAPTER 7

FOLLOWING THE LEADER

ONE OF THE GREATEST THRILLS OF MY LIFE WAS addressing my very own racing team for the first time in February 2002. My friends, I am the co-owner of a NASCAR team. That is not an honorary title, I paid for the right to make that claim. Our car is driven by Kerry Earnhardt, son of the greatest race car driver who ever lived, Dale Earnhardt. We were in Daytona, getting ready for the first race of the season. The morning of the race the team met in our trailer and I gave them a pep talk. We have got to work together, I told them, my voice beginning to rise.

We will work together, I promised, then continued to urge my team to victory, and no matter what happens out there on that track today, we're gonna work together, we're gonna stay together, we're gonna win together! We want to be safe, we want to be smart, we need to trust ourselves. Now I know that a lot is expected of us and I also know that we have the ability to deliver on that; I don't just think that, I know that! I said, I know that. We have a great team, a great driver, a great car. I know the pressure is on us, but we're not going to let that affect us, no we are not, we're gonna go out there . . .

Having spent half my lifetime in locker rooms listening to football coaches prepare teams for games, another half of my life giving inspirational speeches, and another half of my life preparing for moments when I would address my own team, I believed in my ability to help us rise to the occasion. So in that trailer I gave them my greatest speech, my General Patton-before-the-battle speech. Oh, my, it was a beautiful speech. Maybe when we went into that trailer we were just a group of individuals searching for a cause, but when we came out of there we came out as a team, ready to battle for victory, ready to sacrifice for each other; we were a team, prepared to win as a team or if the Good Lord chose, prepared to lose as a team.

Then they went and crashed my car on the twentieth lap.

On the way home I decided that since the General Patton speech didn't work, the next week I'd have to go to my Billy Graham speech. We've faced adversity, my friends, yes, I said, we have visited the pits of despair, we have been to the mountaintop and looked the devil in his burning eyes and . . .

At times in all of our lives we all have been members of a team. The word *team* here meaning a group of people working together toward a common goal. Your high school class was a team. All you people who work for a company are members of a team. If you belong to a club, you're on the team. Your family is a team. In fact, when I was with the Steelers we had so many key players stay together so long we thought of ourselves as a family.

Of course, the biggest difference between professional teams and your family is that if you don't perform well your family can't cut you. You might get booed, but you won't get cut.

Every one of those teams has a leader, the one person in charge, the person who takes the responsibility for turning a group of individuals into one team. For making sure every individual knows his job on the team and performs it to the best of his or her ability.

A leader is simply a person who takes charge and takes responsibility. The greatest military leaders, Washington, Grant, Patton, Montgomery, all had one thing in common. When you see a painting or a photograph of them they are all in the same place: behind their troops. That's probably where the expression "We're behind you all the way" comes from. Because those people never got near the frontlines. The fact is that you don't need to be in front to be the leader. You don't need to yell the loudest or be the strongest. Probably the weakest person physically on the Steelers was head coach Chuck Noll. But we could not possibly have won four Super Bowls without him. He never threw one pass, never gained a single yard, but he was our leader.

Every one of us has leaders in our lives. No matter how successful we become we are all accountable to some people above us. Except maybe being king, for example. David Hill, head of Fox Sports, is my leader. Your boss is definitely a leader. Maybe your husband or your wife is the leader of your family. In some cases your parole officer is—

The fact is there is only one thing a person needs to be a leader. Just one thing. Anybody know what this is?

No, the answer is not "hair." The answer is that the only thing you need to be a leader is followers. You can't be a leader without people following you. What would a band leader be without a band? Just another crazy guy waving his arms through the air.

I became the leader of my racing team the old-fashioned way. I bought it. The fact is that people become leaders in a lot of different ways. Maybe they're born into it, or buy it or they earn it or just take it; it doesn't matter how you get to the position, it's what you do with it.

I've learned the secrets of leadership that I tried to bring home to my racing team from many different leaders. The first leader in my life was my dad. He led through example and intimidation, although admittedly the intimidation part was a lot stronger.

My father was born and raised in Sparta, Tennessee. Now that was definitely the appropriate place for him to be from, because he definitely was a Spartan. Growing up he played football on the West Sparta town team. Those people were tough, they didn't have protective pads. The team had one plastic helmet but, knowing my father, I'm sure he didn't get to use it much. My father had to quit high school to go to work. Years later, though, when he was working full-time as the vice president of his company while raising three boys, he got his high school degree. When he was fifty-five years old he went to night college and is only twenty-two hours shy of his college degree in industrial engineering. He taught me honesty, discipline, and the value of hard work. He taught me to take pride in myself. "Don't ever forget you're carrying my name," he said. "Don't embarrass that name."

If you start something, he said, no matter how tough it is, you finish it. You don't quit. As much as I loved football, there were times growing up when I was ready to quit. Football in the South was a test of manhood, a test of toughness. But looking back on it now, it was barbaric. Practicing twice a day in the heat of a Louisiana summer, no water, running gassers after a two-hour practice, never getting a break. It was brutal. I don't how many times I wanted to quit. But my father would not let me. Just flat out told me I was not allowed to quit. He didn't know I was going to grow up to be a pro football player, there wasn't anything he could do to make that happen, but he knew for certain that I was going to grow up to be a man.

There was never a doubt who the leader was in our family. My father's basic philosophy of leadership was straightforward: Do what I tell you or else. It was definitely hands-on leadership; sometimes it was even belt-on. In our house he was sort of like General Patton, but without the sensitivity. My brother and I lived in fear of that threat, orrrrrr ellllllsee. "Now look what you've done, Terry. Dad's getting ready for an or else."

"Oh no, not an or else!"

One time, I remember, I was in third grade and I wanted to play baseball with my friends. I had a little shabby glove but our next door neighbor, Mr. Robinson, who coached a team of older players, would let me use his glove. Man, that was a beautiful baseball glove. Unfortunately, this time I lost Mr. Robinson's glove. Let me make this clear: I lost his baseball glove. There probably are some fine people out there who don't fully understand the relationship between a boy or man and a baseball glove. A baseball glove is a treasure, an object of affection, a holder of memories—and I lost Mr. Robinson's baseball glove.

It fell off my bike and I spent hours searching for it. It was gone. I was petrified. A few days later Mr. Robinson leaned over the backyard fence and said the most terrifying words I'd ever heard to my dad. "Bill, could you holler at Terry and see if he could bring my glove? I got practice."

When my dad told me to get Mr. Robinson's glove I said, "Yessir," ran right upstairs to my room and started looking in that closet. Basically what I was looking for was an excuse. I didn't know what I was going to do; I knew for sure no one would believe me if I claimed that the glove had committed suicide.

"Terry, hurry up with that glove."

"I'm coming, Dad." Trust me here, people, I wasn't going anywhere. I was in that closet on my hands and knees trying to bargain with God. Listen, God, if you let me find Mr. Robinson's glove I'll . . . I'll dedicate my entire life to being the best person there ever was and I'll never lose another baseball glove . . ."

Suddenly my father yanked me out of that closet. My father was not a parent who believed in sparing the rod. I got the extra-special full rod. Twice—once for losing the glove in the first place and second for lying about it. Experiences like that tend to make you focus a little better. And I guarantee you we followed that man's direction.

Intimidation is definitely one form of leadership, and my father tempered justice with mercy, always being there when his family needed him. But intimidation won't always work. An effective leader learns the strengths and weaknesses of his people and how to get each person to produce his best. Different people respond to different things. I learned that from Chuck Noll. For a time early in my career the Steelers had three talented quarterbacks, myself, Gilliam, and Terry Hanratty. Three very different personalities. We'd all be in the same meeting with Noll but each of us would walk out of it feeling very differently. I'd be whupped, Gilliam would be furious, and Hanratty would be smiling and shaking his head in disbelief.

From the time he was hired in Pittsburgh in 1969 Chuck Noll had the confidence of a leader. What he didn't have was the right followers. Let me put it this way: If General Grant had been leading the Salvation Army instead of the Union Army y'all would be talking real slow. In Noll's first year as the Steelers head coach the team went 1-13. The Steelers had won more games than that the year before—and that coach had been fired. But Chuck Noll had established certain standards. Like a true leader he had set reasonable goals. He knew he wasn't going to win in the National Football League right away. He had a plan.

Then they drafted me. That probably wasn't in his plan. I wanted to be a good follower, I wanted to follow my coach, but I needed a kind hand to lead me. I had come to the great National Football League from the little bitty school of Louisiana Tech. Read a defense? I'd hardly even read a book.

Chuck Noll was a brilliant man. He could talk to you about anything from local politics to golf, airplanes, horses, the best way to lay a concrete floor, but he didn't really understand human behavior. Certain leaders can adjust to their team; Jimmy Johnson is great at that. Bill Parcells is probably the best at it. They have the ability to reach inside different kinds of people to motivate them. They can become whatever they need to be. For a long time Chuck Noll was inflexible. I was lost and I needed someone to build my confidence. A reporter once wrote that when we won our first Super Bowl Chuck Noll celebrated by shaking hands with his wife. That was probably apocryphal. Probably. I respected him, but it took us a long time to get along. We fought. There were times I wanted to hit him. He would yell at me in front of the entire team; one time he fined me $25 for being three minutes late to a pregame meal—because I was standing outside talking to Mr. Rooney, the owner of the team. But the worst moment came during a 1973 preseason exhibition game against the Giants. With less than a minute left in the first half he signaled me to keep the ball on the ground. Run out the clock. With a big strong arm like I had he wanted me to run out the clock? Take a shot at it, I thought, throw that football. I was going to put some points on the scoreboard, take my team to the promised land.

My pass was intercepted and returned for a touchdown.

When we received the kickoff with less than thirty seconds left in the half Noll again signaled for me to keep the football on the ground. Well, shucks, ladies and gentlemen, I already cost us one touchdown by not listening to him, now I had an obligation to make up for that. And I wasn't going to make up for it with a five-yard run. I had to throw that ball.

My pass was intercepted.

When I ran to the sidelines Noll was livid. If I had thought about it, I might have looked way up into the sky and said, "Lord 'member that time we were talking about the lost baseball glove?" But I didn't have time to think, Chuck grabbed me by the facemask and started dragging me around in front of the entire team like an animal, screaming at me. I was humiliated. I was embarrassed.

I was also wrong. I knew that. But by that point Chuck should have realized I was not the kind of player who responded to that kind of treatment. Whether he was right or wrong, he definitely did not achieve his objective.

We battled for most of my career. Chuck was a professor in a coaching position; he understood the intricacies of the game like few people I have ever known. He understood the xs and the os. We were always a well-prepared football team. In his offense the quarterback was supposed to drop back and read the defense by following specific keys. If the middle linebacker had vacated the center, that meant that Lynn Swann became my primary receiver. If Swannie was covered I was supposed to look to John Stallworth coming across the middle. If he was covered that meant Franco Harris coming out of the backfield had to be free. Had to be. It said so right there on the blackboard. I'm sure it all made sense.

But I just threw the ball to the open man. And if the man wasn't quite as open as he needed to be, I scrambled a little bit and then just threw it to him a little harder. There were times after I'd completed a pass to the wrong receiver I'd go to the sidelines and he couldn't even talk to me. He'd be biting his tongue.

But Chuck Noll knew football. He built the Steelers through the draft. Then he designed an offense around the strengths of his players. The Steelers were small but quick. Our linemen weren't as big as other teams' but they were mobile, so our system depended on trapping and pulling. He realized after my rookie season that my strength was throwing the football down the field twenty or thirty yards, so he created the offense to take advantage of that. Leaders don't need to be loved, they need to be respected, and everyone respected Chuck. He wasn't loud, he never did say very much, and he was not comparable to the great Notre Dame coach Knute Rockne giving inspirational speeches. Chuck was the essential modern leader: He had a plan, everything he did from the players he drafted to his offensive strategy was consistent with that plan and he convinced his team that his plan would work. So when he did say something we all knew he was serious about it.

Once, when we were a young and a somewhat inexperienced football team we played the Raiders in Oakland. The great silver-and-black Oakland Raiders. Al Davis's Raiders. John Madden's Raiders. It's not that we were scared of them; nobody reaches that level and is scared. It's just that we didn't believe we could beat them. In our team meeting before we left Pittsburgh Noll reviewed our game strategy—it was a typical meeting—and then added confidently, "The Raiders don't know it yet, but we're going to go out there and beat those sons o' bitches."

All of us have heard boasts like that before: We're gonna sell more insurance policies this year than there are people in the whole world! We're gonna double last year's record-breaking profits—but this year we're gonna do it in only three months or I'm retiring to my villa on Tax Haven Island. Most of the time we don't pay any more attention to it. It has about as much value as a politician's campaign promise. It's just the annual barn-burner.

The difference was that Chuck Noll had never said anything like that before. Chuck had established himself as a no-nonsense direct-to-the-listener speaker. In every situation when he said something he meant it. He'd followed through. He had never given us any reason to doubt him. So when he said we were going to beat the Raiders we believed him. We trusted him. Chuck said we were going to win this game, so we knew we were going to win the game. Who were we to argue with him? He was the coach, we were only the players.

Did it really make a difference on the playing field? Absolutely, it did. We went to Oakland and beat the Raiders.

On the football field the quarterback has to be the leader of the team. There is no dissent permitted in the huddle. But I definitely would never claim that I was the leader of the Pittsburgh Steelers. I wasn't that type of player. Off the field I was pretty much a loner; I didn't hang out with my teammates, I didn't drink, I didn't chase after wom—I didn't drink. But what I earned from my teammates was their respect. On the field I performed. I did my job. When I got hit I got up and I didn't complain. I tried to get everyone involved in the offense. I listened to my teammates' suggestions. I always followed Chuck Noll's instructions except for those times when I didn't. And I always accepted responsibility for my actions.

Every leader I have ever known has accepted responsibility for his or her own actions. When something goes wrong a leader doesn't blame it on somebody else. Believe me, I have heard all kinds of excuses in my life: It was the teacher's fault I failed that test; she didn't ask the questions that I knew the answers to. It was the customer's fault that we didn't sell more peanut butter; have you ever seen so many people who have no taste? I would've caught that pass but these two defensive backs were bearing down on me and my life insurance expired last Thursday and I forgot to renew it. And maybe the best excuse of them all: It's all your fault, you listened to me!

I've made only one excuse in my playing career, but I didn't make it until I'd retired. I told people that I didn't play well inside domed stadiums because I couldn't see well. I wear glasses. Inside a dome it always seemed hazy to me and my depth perception isn't very good. So I was a poor judge of distances; I either threw too hard or not hard enough.

There is a very good reason why I finally admitted that. But if I explained why I made that excuse I would be making an excuse for making an excuse. And I believe there is no excuse for doing that. People make mistakes. But the mark of a leader is accepting responsibility for them.

My father and Chuck Noll were authoritative leaders. "Or else" leaders. But the owner of the Steelers, Art Rooney, led by the nature of his personality. He was the kind of person people just naturally wanted to follow. There is a word for that—and that word is not *rich*. That word is *charisma*. He was a nice, decent person who made you want to work hard for him. He was always so encouraging, so supportive, that I just didn't want to disappoint him.

Supposedly Mr. Rooney paid his entrance fee to the brand-new National Football League with money he'd won at the racetrack. Maybe. I don't doubt he was at the track. He loved horses as much as I did. One time, I remember, I boarded two horses at his stables and when the time came to settle the bill we had a minor dispute about it. I think it had something to do with him wanting me to pay for it. It was certainly no big deal, it was one of those things that friends joke about for a long time. Some time later I was in his office—he wasn't there—and I had to use his telephone. Mr. Rooney had a small statue of praying hands on his desk and when I finished my call—to make a point—I took out a one-dollar bill to pay for the call and stuck it in that statue.

Apparently that's what the statue was praying for. Mr. Rooney left it there. To make his point. As anyone who knew Mr. Rooney would explain, that was a remarkable thing. He never left a dollar on the table. But every time I went into his office that dollar bill was still there, still stuck in that statue. The amazing thing was that this was decades before I started doing TV commercials for the cut-rate phone company 10-10-220; commercials that focus on what you can do with the one dollar you save by using this phone service. For example, you could stick it in Art Rooney's statue.

I loved Art Rooney.

The leader of Fox Sports is David Hill. Maybe the one thing that most Americans have in common is that we all have to deal with—the boss. Like everybody else, I have a boss. But unlike a lot of people I can say publicly anything I want to say about my boss. Because my boss gave me permission to do that. That's my job, my boss told me, to state my opinions. Fortunately, I have a fine opinion of my boss.

A lot of people believe that because I'm a popular TV personality I don't have to worry about my job. But trust me, at some point in the future there will be one Sunday when I won't be on that show—and you know what will happen? The show will go on the air just like it did the week before or the season before. My chair will be there, it just won't be me sitting in it. Where's Terry, viewers will say the first week, we miss him. The second week viewers will be saying, What happened to what's his name? And by the third week they'll decide, You know this new guy is a lot smarter and funnier than old—you know who I mean.

The reality is that you can fire the rooster and the sun will still come up the next morning. I am replaceable. And like everybody else who has a job I am accountable to someone above me. That someone is my boss. Or as I like to refer to him, my wonderful boss. David Hill. I have worked out my own special strategy for dealing with David Hill. I am always very honest with him and I know he respects me for it. I honestly tell him exactly what I believe he wants to hear. I suppose there are people who might accuse me of sucking up to the boss. And to those people I say, so what? If you can't flatter your boss, who in the world can you flatter? He's the boss.

We do play golf on occasion, for example, and you should hear me out on the course. I think it is fair to say that I'm an embarrassment to my unborn great-grandchildren; Oh, my goodness, David, what a beautiful swing, oh that was beautiful; man, if you'd of hit that ball it would have gone a real long way. Or, Hey, David, that is some incredible golf shot; I've never even seen a pro hit a shot like that. Wow, a three-fairway cross-shot.

When Fox won the rights to broadcast NFL football David Hill was put in the same position Chuck Noll had been in when he took over the Steelers. He had to build an entire operation from scratch. The main difference was that Hill was an Australian who had been working in London and knew very little about American football. It took the same kind of leadership that Noll had exhibited; a vision, a work ethic, and the ability to hire the right people and delegate authority to them.

One thing David Hill had going for him was that he wasn't

hindered by too much knowledge. Which of course has always been one of my major attributes. Not being too familiar with the existing pregame shows David didn't feel a need to copy them. What he had was the prime ingredient of all effective leaders: confidence in his own ideas. Right or wrong, he believed in them and he was going to succeed or fail by implementing them. His most revolutionary idea was to expand the pregame show from the traditional half hour to a full hour. An hour long pregame show? David Hill said people reacted as though he was crazy, "Apparently since Moses came down from the mount with the tablets," he says, "the Eleventh Commandment had been 'Thou shalt have a half-hour pregame show.'"

But Hill had another thing that every successful leader has, the support of his boss, the man paying the bills. Like Chuck Noll had Art Rooney, David Hill had Rupert Murdoch. Hill's vision of the show was two good friends sitting down in the stadium an hour before the game. They talk a little football, maybe argue, maybe make a little bet but basically they enjoy each other's company; they're interested in the game without treating it as a religious spectacle and they want to have fun.

That was the way he envisioned the show. Of course, to bring his vision of two guys talking football to reality he had to hire four men. Hey, leaders don't have to be good with math. Leaders can hire accountants.

I was the first on-air personality he hired. He'd seen me on the CBS pregame show with Greg Gumbel. The half-hour CBS show. I'd like to think he hired me because of my perspicuity, my raffish charm, my well-hewn good looks, my introspective understanding of the inner workings of the National Football League, my savoir faire, and my ability to speak good English.

Yes, I definitely would like to think that. However, if I did I would be wrong. "I'd heard a whole bunch of stuff about Terry," my very own boss told a journalist, "most of it negative. No one could understand him because of his accent, and the way he presented it he didn't seem to know much about football.

"But I was watching tapes and at one time Terry got up from the desk and walked across the set to illustrate something on the Telestrator and in those three paces there was just such style, assuredness, and positive energy. And then he stood and talked and I understood it and he did it with a smile and he was having fun and looking forward to the game. And I knew he was the guy I wanted."

Now let me interpret that for you: This Australian from England working in America was first impressed by the way I walked—and then he was impressed by the fact that he understood Southern. Maybe he even liked my barnyard metaphors. But that's how he came to be my boss.

Like Noll, David Hill could be as tough as he needed to be. One of the things I admired about Chuck was his dedication to winning. When a player no longer fit into his plan, when a player could no longer perform to his level of excellence, he didn't hesitate to cut that player loose. I understood that; I understood it completely just about right up until the time it was my turn. When David Hill was putting together the staff for the show one of the first people he hired was the producer. But after working with this producer for several weeks he realized that man's vision of the show was different from his own. That producer wanted to do a more traditional football show. David Hill fired him. That was actually a pretty gutsy thing to do. Most leaders will never admit they've made a mistake. No one ever heard Attila the Hun admit he'd invaded the wrong country. A lot of experienced people doubted David Hill could produce a network-quality pregame show and football telecast, and firing his producer could have been seen as just a tiny little bit of panic. An early admission of failure.

I do know people who read or hear criticism in the press or on television and immediately react to it. They make changes to try to please those few critics rather than doing what they believe is right. If there is one thing at which I am an expert it is not reacting to criticism. When I was hosting my own morning show the producers asked me kindly to stop sweating so much. Well, that request made me so nervous I just started sweating more.

Real leaders have convictions. David Hill hired Scotty Ackerson and allowed him to produce the show. Scotty Ackerson has been my boss since I joined the program—which allows me to say meaningfully and with great pleasure that Scotty Ackerson is also one of the finest golfers it has been my privilege to have ever played a round with.

It must be very difficult to be an effective leader, otherwise they wouldn't keep publishing all those books revealing the amazing leadership secrets of everyone from Attila to the retired president of General Electric. And people must want to know these secrets otherwise they wouldn't buy the books. It seems to me, though, that being a successful leader can be pretty simple: Start by establishing your goals and how you expect to accomplish them. Take responsibility for your own actions. Hire competent people and allow them to do the job you hired them to do. Make only those rules that are necessary and be consistent in their application. Be as tough as you need to be when you need to be tough. Treat the people working for you as you would like to be treated.

And don't worry about your people who sweat the small stuff. As well as the big stuff.

CHAPTER 8

THERE'S ALWAYS TIME FOR A GOOD TIME

I FEEL IT IS MY OBLIGATION TO WARN YOU THAT THERE is danger, my friends, serious danger, to be found on the golf course. Particularly if I'm driving the golf cart. A dear friend of mine, Dick Compton, went flying out of the cart one day when I made a hard left, body-slamming him on the number six fairway at Cottonwood. This was a terrible thing to have happen, as I was having a career round. "My shoulder," Dick yelled, "my shoulder."

I looked over at him. His shoulder was pointed toward the sky at an extreme angle. "Dick," I said urgently, "Dick, can you go on? I'm having a great round!"

"I'm hurting, Terry," he said, "maybe you'd better drive me home."

Considering that, I said as I reached into my golf bag, "I don't know about that. I'm not having a good day driving at all. Let's see how far we can get with a two-iron."

Old Dick laughed the whole way to the hospital emergency room, where his injury was diagnosed as a completely separated shoulder. From the look of these X rays, the doctor told him, "It looks like you've been playing golf with Terry Brad-shaw."

Sometimes we all work so hard we forget exactly why we're working so hard. We get so caught up trying to earn enough money to enjoy our leisure time or fix up the house that we have no time at all to enjoy the house. Believe me, that is one of the biggest problems of my life.

The single most important suggestion I can make to you is take time to enjoy yourself. I know that sounds simple. It sounds that way because it is simple. But I'm telling you that the single best thing you can do to improve your very own life is slow down a little and take time to do those things you really enjoy. It doesn't matter what that is. If you love bowling, go bowling. If you're an ice fisherman, go catch some ice. Take time to work on your hobby. And if you just like to watch TV, please watch *NFL Sunday* on Fox noon Eastern Standard Time during football season.

I'm very fortunate, there are a lot of things that I can do to relax. But probably the thing that brings me the most pleasure is the magnificent game of golf. Golf is a great game of luck and skill and intelligence that forces you to get in touch with your inner self. And as I learned from playing golf, my inner self is pretty darn nasty. That inner self has a bad temper.

In high school I set the national record for javelin throw-ing. I remember in school when we took math courses some-one would always ask the teacher, Teacher, why do we have to know math? And the teacher would say, Because, Terry, some-day the bills are going to come to your house and you have to be able to figure them out. Javelin chucking raised a similar question for me. I couldn't understand how throwing a long straight metal pole as far as I could would ever be valuable to me in later life.

Of course, that was long before I discovered golf. Thanks to my high school training I can throw a golf club a great distance. I have left a trail of broken and discarded clubs on golf courses all over the country. While I've thrown all my clubs, mostly I throw putters; I'll bet I have $5,000 worth of putters rusting in lakes. Once I threw my whole bag in the lake and just walked off the course. That teacher was absolutely right about math, incidentally; I didn't pay attention so I don't have the slightest idea how many clubs I've broken. One day I got so mad I took three clubs and snapped them. A record that stands as my personal best. I've banged clubs into the ground, against the golf cart, against the wall.

Which is why I play golf to relax.

The fact is that there are few things in life that I enjoy more than being outside on a golf course with some good friends. The key thing for me is to not take it very seriously. Because if I did take it seriously it would drive me crazy. That devious little white ball just lays there, looking so innocent, so easy to hit. Just stand there and whack it and say, oh my, isn't that beautiful. But as all golfers know, that's just the lure. What that ball really is doing lying there is taunting you, daring you to hit it where you want it to go. That ball is pitting you against the greatest enemy you will ever face: your own mind. Once you get down the basic skills golf is basically a psychological game that you play against yourself—and usually lose. The ability of that little white ball to drive otherwise sane and even happy human beings to despair is extraordinary.

Football is a game of reaction. After the ball is snapped you have to allow your instincts, your experience, and your talent to take control. There is no time to think. Golf is a mental game. That's what makes it so tough. If you've played often enough, when you make a mistake you know exactly what you've done wrong—the challenge is to quit doing it. Just like marriage.

I began playing golf at a par 3—a short course—while I was in college. I was a very strong athlete, but I was a terrible golfer. I couldn't hit that ball straight at all. It made me so miserable I'd have to go right back and fail again the next day. I really started to learn how to play when I was in training camp with the Steelers in Latrobe, Pennsylvania. I'd go over to Arnold Palmer's Driving Range and hit balls for hours.

During the season we had off on Mondays to recuperate from the game on Sunday. Every Monday morning, I mean every Monday, I played golf. I never missed a Monday. Even if I had been injured during the game I would hobble around the course. If I couldn't walk I'd crawl. People would see me crawling around the course and say, Golly that old boy has some guts. Then I'd kind of struggle to my knees and from my knees I'd drive the ball about fifty yards—straight into the rough— and I'd be so angry I'd throw my club straight down the fairway about seventy yards. And those same people would see me throw that club and they'd say, Sure, why didn't he throw it like that yesterday?

The real key to my success on the golf course is cheating. I have rarely played an honest round of golf in my life. I don't try to hide it either. I cheat, and announcing that before I start makes the day far more enjoyable. I'm good at cheating too. I can land on the green, pick up my ball and mark the spot to allow someone else to putt first, and by the time I put down my ball I will be a minimum ten feet closer to the pin.

I tell people that the only reason I cheat on the golf course is to get a better score. That's not exactly true. I cheat because I'm playing to have fun with my friends, and I know that they are going to cheat too. In fact, when we tee it up on the first hole we always say there will be no cheating permitted until the first ball is struck.

Least I admit I cheat. I know this will be hard to accept, but incredibly, there actually are some people who cheat at golf and don't admit it! Those people are generally known as—pretty much everybody. Let's be honest. Who among us has never cheated on a golf course?

Put your hand down, Jesus.

Everybody cheats, and when I catch them they always use the same lame excuse, "But I learned that from you, Terry." There are ways to detect efforts at cheating. This happens to be an area on which I consider myself an expert. For example, when you're riding in a cart with someone whose ball is fifty yards farther from the green than yours, and they politely say, "Hey don't worry about it, I'll take you all the way to your ball first"—that is a dead giveaway.

The kind of golfers to be wary of are those people who never lose a golf ball. I don't want to mention any names, my brother Craig, but there are some people who have never lost a single golf ball in their life. Some people, certainly not my brother Craig, could find a golf ball dropped from 10,000 feet into the rain forest. It is the most amazing thing no one has ever seen. These people will disappear into the rough; you can't even see them, and suddenly a hand holding a golf ball will pop out of the bushes and Cra—they will scream, Found it!

However, I never do cheat when we're playing for money. I'm not going to go into the rough and suddenly find a lost ball in a great position or forget to count a stroke, not when there is money changing hands. So if we ever play golf together for money you don't even have to bother watching me when I go into the rough or get a bad lie. Trust me on that, my good friend, you just trust me.

The best round I've ever had was a 4 under par 68, although in reality it probably would have been about a 74 because I bumped the ball around in the rough and improved my lie. I was playing in Tucson, Arizona. For all you nongolfers, improving my lie doesn't mean I just told something that wasn't exactly true a little more convincingly, it means that I moved the ball from the spot where it was lying on the ground. My real lies don't need improving, I got them down real well.

I have had three holes-in-one. Three. And here is the truth of it all: You can't cheat on a hole-in-one. My first hole-in-one was the most amazing golf shot I have ever seen. I was playing with my close friend from high school Tommy Spinks, and we had a $5-a-hole bet going. We were playing the ninth hole in Cottonwood, Texas. It was about 170 yards with a small lake in front and traps on either side. There was a slight breeze blowing from behind. The hardest decision in golf is choosing the correct club, that club that will give you exactly the distance you estimate. I was holding a 5-iron, but after considering the distance, the wind velocity, the chances that I actually was going to hit the ball straight, I asked Tommy to hand me a 4-iron.

Here's another important piece of advice: Never ask the person with whom you're betting to help you. Sure, Tommy said, handing me a 3-iron, here it is. My swing was picture perfect, but that picture was R-rated. I sculled the ball, I topped it, I hit a low line drive. That ball hit the water and skipped once, twice and then hit the bank and popped into the air, landed on the green, and rolled into the cup. The toughest thing about the entire shot was acting as if I wasn't stunned. Oh yeah, just like I practiced it. I figured I'd bounce it off the water into the bank and slide it down the green to the hole.

It was the Immaculate Reception of golf. Tommy started running toward the hole screaming and yelling. He didn't know whether to take the credit for it or the blame; he did know it was going to cost him his $5!

My other two holes-in-one came on consecutive days on the same hole at the Cherry Hills Country Club in Pittsburgh. I never saw either one of them go in the hole. Both days were wet, hazy, and overcast. On a Monday morning I hit a high fly into the haze and we lost track of it. Never saw it land. We searched for about twenty minutes, I was about to give up and drop another ball when someone glanced into the hole and started shouting. The next morning I hit a similar shot, again we couldn't find it, again we looked for it. Nobody even bothered looking in the hole because we knew it would be impossible to have done it two days in a row.

Oh, my goodness gracious. Oh, my. Thank you, thank you very much. Which is how I have as many holes-in-one as I do ex-wives.

I definitely remember the worst round of golf I've ever played. My good friend and attorney Jack Carlisle and I played several of the great golf courses of Scotland. Actually, mis-played is probably a more accurate term. But one morning we tried to play Carnoustie, which many people believe to be one of the best courses in the world. The people there told me golf had been played on that course since the sixteenth century, which did not surprise me at all. In fact, I think I met this man in the rough who looked like he'd been looking for his ball since maybe 1750. This course is so famous that people fly to Scotland from around the world just to play one round. My question is, why? That was the hardest course I'd ever seen. Why would you fly thousands of miles just to be humiliated? I shot a 139. And if I hadn't cheated on the eighteenth hole I would have shot a 150, give or take 10 strokes.

The famed eighteenth hole is a 487-yard par 4. The wind was at my back when I teed off and I just got into my drive. It soared, it was gorgeous, straight down the fairway I'd estimate 375 yards. It was the longest drive of my life. I had never realized I had that much power, that I could hit a ball so long and so true. After a terrible round, even one shot can make you feel proud. For my second shot I decided to go for the green. I took my 7-iron and hit it clean—and the wind caught that ball too—and carried it maybe 260 yards, way over the green, into a parking lot. Last time I saw that ball it was bouncing toward London.

I may have hit one drive even longer than that, but I'll never know for certain. One night a long time ago, a long, long time ago, much longer than the statute of limitations, I was in New York City with my producer at CBS, Terry O'Neill. It was probably about 2 A.M. During the dinner we'd had a few drinks and talked quite a bit about golf and had a few more drinks and O'Neill had been critical of my game, particularly my ability to hit a 1-iron. So as we walked back to the car, which was parked on Madison Avenue, I saw he had his golf bag in the backseat. "That's it," I said boldly, "gimme the one-iron."

"What are you gonna do?" he asked.

"I'm gonna show you that I can whomp that sucker."

See, this is where O'Neill made his big mistake. He thought I was kidding. He—

I just want to pause here and remind everyone not to try this at home, and also not to try this when not at home. Thank you, now back to my story.

—he gave me the club, a ball, and a tee. I wedged that tee into a crack in the sidewalk and took my stance. I waited till there wasn't a car in the distance. Now, there are people who will tell you how hard it is to drive in New York City, but I would not be among them. I hit that ball cleanly, whoosshhhhhh. I hit a rising liner straight down Madison Avenue. That ball just took off, bounced once, and disappeared straight down that street, never to be seen again.

I think the reason that golf relaxes me is that I don't put any pressure on myself to perform. Most of us have certain expectations of ourselves at work, at home, and if we don't achieve them we get sad or depressed. When I play golf my only expectation is that at the end of eighteen holes I will have played eighteen holes. Even with my limited math skills I know that to be true.

I have faced the reality that my skills on the golf course are equaled only by my skills as a motion picture actor. I treat the game of golf with all the seriousness it deserves. That's why I created the Bradshaw Rules of Golf, or officially Bradshaw's

Expanded Rules of Golf. When I play golf the Bradshaw Rules are always in effect. The first rule is that no matter what you shoot on the first hole, in my case anything from a double bogie to a quadruple bogie, you are going to par the hole. You can slice and dice your way to the green, but on that scorecard you are going to have a par. This guarantees that you will get your round off to a good start. I put this rule into effect because too often we would ruin an otherwise good round by getting to the course too late to warm up and take a 6 or 11 on the first hole.

The Bradshaw Rules permit cheating and noise shots. A noise shot is a shot that you haven't hit very well, after which you say, "I don't know what that noise was, but it really bothered me so I need to hit it again." The "wasp" variation requires you to hit, then slap at the air and say, "Dang, that was the biggest wasp I have ever seen. You guys ever see anything like that?"

They are officially known as "the expanded rules" because they're flexible. They expand to meet just about any situation. Excuses for taking a second shot are an important part of the expanded rules. Good excuses might include: My foot slipped on the ice. Someone was thinking too loudly. It's Monday. Oh, man, my Butkus is killing me. It's Tuesday. As you might expect, we're not too picky about excuses.

Certainly one of the most important expanded rules is that only one pole whupping per round is permitted. Pole whupping is my prime psychological weapon on a golf course. I discovered it while playing in a weekend Pro-Am in Fort Worth. Jack Carlisle and I were in a foursome that included a doctor from Shreveport. On Saturday we were playing the sixth hole.

I had already won or tied the hole, but the doctor was no more than three feet from the cup and insisted on putting out. He wouldn't take a gimme, he needed to putt that ball. Okay, I figured, you want to putt so badly, I'll help you putt that badly. So real quiet-like I took the flagpole and nonchalantly moved around behind him, dooo-do-dooo, and when he leaned over and carrrrrefully drew back his putter to hit the ball I took that pole and I whupped that flag right over the top of his head. Bbbplaplaplapplapplapplapplapplapplapplapp! The man putted that ball at least forty yards. Then he dived onto the green.

I don't know, maybe I shouldn't have been surprised how angry he was. He screamed and yelled and cursed at me. He marched over to the golf cart, picked off my bag and threw it onto the ground, drove back to the clubhouse, got in his car, and drove straight home to Shreveport. All because I'd pole whupped him.

I just stood there in shock watching him leave. I thought he would understand that I would never do something like that to a person I didn't like.

But that day flag whupping was born. Now I am specifically advising people not to pole whup unless they have been professionally trained. You have to be extremely careful. Under no circumstances, for example, do you want to use a metal pole because if you're just a little bit off with your timing you can hit someone in the back of the head and knock them out cold. Seriously, that's a real problem. Then you have to drag them around the course for the rest of the round.

Fiberglass poles are preferred by experienced whuppers. They got a real nice plapplaplap to them. Pole whupping is not as easy as it sounds. The key to achieving a successful whup is subtlety. After pulling the pole out of the hole you might just stand on the green a few seconds. Then, as the putter is setting up, ease into a position behind him, always making sure the sun is not at your back because the putter will see your shadow. Take a baseball batter's stance behind the putter, standing sideways. Your feet should be a comfortable distance apart, balance is important. When the putter finally brings back his club to putt, step forward with your left side, keep your elbows in, your hips flexed, and remember to follow through. I just can't emphasize enough the importance of a clean follow-through. Make sure you start out with the pole parallel to the ground and swing nice and level. If you swing up, there's a chance you'll pull a muscle on your left side, a common injury.

This is as close to contact golf as you will ever get. I have been pole whupped by my brother Craig and I promise you, that sound coming toward you is frightening. It sounds like a helicopter coming in for a landing on your head. It definitely takes your heartbeat away.

The thing that I do best on the golf course is have fun. Golf serves an important purpose for me; it allows me to relax, it provides a means for me to just get away from the pressures of daily life, hit a few balls, miss a few balls, throw a few clubs, and be with my friends.

I also truly love fishing. I've been fishing pretty much my whole life and I've never yet thrown a single pole in anger. Not only don't I keep score in fishing, I usually don't even keep the fish. Unless I'm planning to cook and eat the fish, I usually catch and release. I'm mostly a freshwater fisherman; I just like to grab a pole and throw a hook into a lake. I don't consider fishing an intellectual challenge between me and the fish. I don't feel like I've outsmarted a fish when I catch it. To me, it's just an easy way to spend quiet, peaceful time. I just like to stand on the bank watching my cork bobbing up and down and relax.

There is no cheering in fishing. I've never seen anyone get upset enough to punch a fish. I've never known anybody who cheats in fishing. For me, fishing is soul work. A time for meditation. A release. It is just about the only thing I'll do by myself. I don't really care if I catch anything or not. The object of fishing, for me, isn't necessarily to catch fish, but rather to find peace. Fishing fills the same purpose for me as knitting does for other people, or carpentry, or any kind of hobby: It's something you do to do. It provides a necessary bit of balance in life. Each of us needs to find that one thing in our lives that gives us the opportunity to just sit back and reflect. Fishing allows me to free up my mind so I can think and maybe solve some problems and sometimes even create.

I've probably raised more fish than I've caught. One year I drained and dredged a small pond on my ranch and built a lake. I stocked it with about five hundred four- and five-inch stripers. Man, I would just turn on the feeders and watch them zoom across that lake. I just loved watching them. About two years later my father asked me how big my fish were.

I didn't have the slightest idea. We went down to the lake with some ultralight line and tried to catch one. We didn't land one of them. Turned out I raised some smart fish. And big, they probably averaged around three pounds.

Trout fishing has never interested me. The problem with

trout fishing is you've got to find just the right stream, which most often means traveling somewhere with a lot of equipment. And that's not something I want to do when I can just walk out my front door and throw a line in Ole Lake Bradshaw. To me, that would be like having to go to Australia to knit a wool sweater because that's where the best sheep are sheared.

On occasion I've gone deep-sea fishing, but that requires too much gear and the fish are too big and strong. I enjoy being on a boat, though, and I've had boats most of my adult life. Little boats, always little boats. The very first thing I bought when I got drafted by the Steelers was a little fishing boat with a twenty-five-horsepower motor. I was so proud of that boat, though admittedly I didn't know much about it. The day I bought it I couldn't wait to get it in the water. Tony Maceto was our line coach at Louisiana Tech, and he loved fishing as much as I did. The first opportunity we had we put my boat on a trailer and drove thirty miles to the nearest lake. We put that boat in the water and then Tony said to me, "Where's the gas tank?"

Gas tank? Don't all motors have gas tanks? I got back in my car and drove thirty miles to the boat dealership and got a tank full of gas and then drove all the way back. We finally got the boat in the water and Tony asked me, can you handle the trolling motor?

Trolling motor? I didn't know anything about trolling motors. All I could do was make us go in circles; big circles, small circles, but always circles. "Whew, Tony," I said to him, "I never knew fishing could make you so dizzy."

I never capsized a boat. I have filled a few up with water, though. One time when I was about fourteen years old my dad and I went out on a lake to fish for bass. He had a ten-foot-long mustard yellow boat. It couldn't have weighed more than twenty pounds. We put our gear in it and sat down and that boat rode low in the water. I rowed. I paddled us right across the lake to the far bank. One thing fishermen know: Fish are always on the other side of the lake. It doesn't matter what side you're on, the fish are on the other side. I paddled, how you doing, Dad, hope you're having a good time.

Thank you, Son, just keep paddling.

We got to the far bank just as a summer storm came up. Either the lake was rising or the boat was sinking, but I noticed it was getting closer. If we moved at all, if we tilted the boat just a bit, water started pouring in. We were sitting in a boat filling up with water. That lake was twenty feet deep in places. In my mind I was swimming for shore, desperate to make it. My dad didn't seem to be worried about it. How you doing, Dad?

Fine, Son, but those fish must be away on vacation. Eventually the storm passed and my father suggested real casually like, Son, why don't you paddle us on back across the lake. Whooooosshhhh, I had us across that lake in minutes.

There are people who believe there is real strategy in fishing. Here's my strategy: Put some food fish like on the end of a hook and toss it in the water. Keep it simple.

I've been hunting most of my life. I'm comfortable in the woods, I can find my way home, but I don't particularly like to hunt. I don't like to kill things. Second, when you're hunting you have to be real quiet; you can't move and you can't talk. Not move? Not talk? Me? I rest my case. If I stood still and didn't make a sound for more than thirty seconds my momma would have the emergency medical people on the way.

Just about everyone in my family—except me—loves to hunt. Truthfully, though, if you release a couple of wild divorce lawyers up in the hills I might find the enjoyment in it. I grew up hunting. When I was a little boy my dad would take us pheasant hunting. We always went opening day of hunting season; we knew it was opening day because the temperature was always in the single digits. But, Dad, it's 4 degrees outside.

It's a dry cold, Son, get dressed.

One time we drove to Mr. K. D. Morris's house to go hunting with him on his land. Mr. Morris was a pig farmer. He had about forty huge hogs in a pen bordered by a line of big cedar trees that acted as a wind break. So while my dad was talking to Mr. Morris I walked over to see the pigs. I felt something hit my shoulder, then something else hit my hunting hat; I looked up and those trees were covered with pheasants. I'm not exaggerating, there must have been hundreds of pheasants. Well, I couldn't wait to tell my dad. I ran back to the farmhouse and started pulling on him, "Dad, Dad . . ."

"Just a minute, Son, can't you see I'm talking here."

"Gary," I told my brother, "there's at least a thousand pheasants right outside." Gary went with me and he couldn't believe it either. We both went running back and started pulling on our dad. Finally, we dragged my father outside.

The hunting season began officially at noon. At five before noon those pheasants took flight. The sky was filled with pheasants. I think the limit was two or three; we shot eighty-seven. I'm not exaggerating except maybe a little. We filled up the back of the station wagon with birds. We were way over the limit. This was a very bad example for my dad to be setting for his sons. I don't think he realized the impact this would have later in my life. It definitely left scars. As a matter of fact, now that I think on it, this is probably the reason I cheat in golf! In fact, I'm certain it is. And if you want to go ahead and cheat, you can blame it on my dad too.

We took the back roads home. We were cleaning birds all night, we had piles of feathers. But we found one bird, a quail, that we had just winged. When we got home we turned it loose in our basement. Every morning my dad would wake up and whistle and that quail in the basement would whistle right back. Unfortunately, one night it got real cold outside, too cold for the bird dogs, and my father made the mistake of putting them in the basement.

You'd think that quail would've whistled for help. My dad could still be whistling today—but he isn't going to get an answer.

It seems to me that the real reason most people hunt is to have a story. So when they go to work Monday morning and someone asks, What'd you do this weekend, Claude? Claude can tell them, took my boy hunting. Yep, we went up into the mountains. Bear country. Big bear country. Just missed a couple of big bears too. Found their tracks. They were still warm, that's how close we came to getting killed and eaten by bears.

I learned how to tell a good hunting story back in Hall Summit. The men in my family would come in from hunting quail or squirrels and while they cleaned them they'd be telling the story of the hunt. Smartest durn squirrel I have ever seen. If they had a Squirrel Hall of Fame his picture'd be up there. Albert Ein-

squirrel. He was disguised as a skunk. This squirrel laid a trap for me; I'm telling you the truth now, boy, if I hadn't outsmarted him he'd be busy cleaning me right now . . .

I'm sure that's where I got my story-telling ability. Which reminds me of the time my teammate Moon Mullins and I were invited to hunt pheasant in Pittsburgh. I got this gorgeous twelve-gauge Browning and we drove out to a hunting lodge. Here's what really happened: The owner of this lodge had fattened up these birds so they couldn't fly. Instead, they jumped, and you'd shoot them on the jump. I've never seen anything like it. They were just walking around, they were not the slightest bit scared; we had to kind of kick them to make them jump. Jump! Boom. Gotcha. Nice shot, Terry.

There was a little dirt road and there must have been two hundred quail at a feeding station there. We walked in among them, scattering them, "Com'on shoo, shoo. Get on up there so I can shoot your ass." They were thirty-pound pheasant, five-pound quail. We got two pheasant. I think I killed one with the butt of my gun and accidentally stepped on another one. But we came home with meat. Then we were going to eat them. I never hunt animals I can't eat. "How we gonna cook 'em?" I asked Moon.

"Fry 'em," he said.

"You ever fried a pheasant?" I asked. He hadn't. "Well, neither have I. How tough can it be?"

By the time I got done cooking this thirty-pound pheasant it weighed a good eight ounces. When we bit into it, the bones crumbled. There was smoke all over my apartment. I even ruined the skillet. We end up going out for Chinese food.

That's what actually happened. But this is the story I am

going to tell. Moon and I got up to the mountain early and started climbing. It had rained all night and rocks were sliding down the hill and one time we had to leap out of the way of this boulder. It seemed like we climbed for hours and never saw a bird.

See where I'm going with this?

But finally we reached a comfortable place and settled in. We sat completely silent for a long time. We didn't even dare breathe. Poor Moon turned so blue, I almost gave him mouth-to-mouth but I was afraid people might talk. Finally two birds passed overhead flying at about five thousand feet. Naturally it was an impossible shot, but I figured if I got that bullet up high enough at just the right angle, as it came down the force of gravity combined with the curvature of the earth would enable me to hit that bird from the top . . .

Then Moon and I used some flint we'd found to light a fire and roasted those birds over an open spit. The most delicious meat I'd ever tasted.

That's the story I tell.

Hunting is just not relaxing to me. Maybe because I don't particularly enjoy it, I'm not particularly good at it. One time when I still had my ranch in Louisiana deer season was opening and my oldest brother Gary wanted to hunt. I had some deer stands, places up in trees where you sit and wait for deer to wander in range, on the back side of the place. I agreed to go with him. So on Sunday night I flew back from Los Angeles after doing the TV show and met him at my ranch. I was pretty tired but, just like you're supposed to, we got up before sunrise Monday morning, ate breakfast, and talked about the hunt. Boone and Crockett is a scoring system used to rate deer, and we anticipated bagging a B & C monster. This was definitely going to be our day. I intended to drag something out of the field that day. It's a man thing.

We drove on out to the stands. I put Gary in one stand and climbed up into another one. I had my .300 magnum elephant gun with me. If I see a deer coming down, that deer is history. Even if I miss him, that gun is so powerful it'll scare it to death.

I was sitting up in this deer stand watching the sun come up. It was a gorgeous fall day. Gary was out of sight, so I would look to my left, look to my right, look behind me, take a nap. I'd wake, look to the right, look to the left, look behind me, go back to sleep. After about three hours of this I woke up, looked to my left, looked to my right, looked behind me—and there he was, the King of All Deer, the white-tail buck of the year. His rack, his antlers, looked like it was four feet wide, twelve points. This was the biggest deer I had ever seen. This was a B & C. This was my trophy. This deer was so big that after I'd shot it I would never have to go deer hunting again, because I could always say, "No sense going again, I'm never gonna find a bigger deer."

Very slowly I lifted my rifle. I eased the scope up to my eye. That deer was standing absolutely still in my crosshairs. I grasped that rifle firmly and squeezed the trigger. BOOM!

That rifle recoiled and hit me right in the face. I dropped the gun to the ground. I had a hole between my eyes where the scope hit me. Blood was pouring out of my face. I thought I was bleeding to death; my nose was broken. My ear was ringing. The loss of blood was making me woozy.

But I've just killed the world's biggest buck.

I started climbing down out of the tree, but there was so much blood on the steps that I slipped and just went brpbrp-brpbrpbrp down that ladder, banging my chin the whole way down. Imagine a cartoon as Road Runner falls down a ladder, slapping his beak against every step. I hit the ground and rolled over. I was hurtin', I mean I was hurtin'—but it was worthwhile. I finally got my Boone and Crockett.

I leaned my gun against the tree and started staggering around. Suddenly Gary comes down the path. He sees me covered in blood. "Oh, my God, T," he screamed, "how did you shoot yourself!" He was close to panicking; it's not too often the deer wins.

"How bad is my head?" I asked him, "Is my nose straight?"

He hesitated, tilting his head to check. "About usual," he said. "We gotta get you to the doctors, get you stitched up."

"Gary," I said excitedly, "Gary, I got the biggest deer you've ever seen in your life. Twelve-point at least. Maybe more. You gotta go get him."

Gary followed my direction a little bit into the woods. Then he got on his hands and knees and crawled a few feet, then pulled out the body of the sorriest-looking, mangiest little bitty deer. It couldn't have weighed more than forty pounds. "Here's your Boone and Crockett," he said.

This is exactly what happens when you give a nearsighted hunter a gun. As we figured out, that deer was standing under a tree—and those branches looked just like antlers to me. So I got me a deer—and a tree. And I also got twelve stitches in my head and a broken nose.

For Gary, this was the beginning of a classic hunting story, the story of Terry's Boone and Crockett.

Gardening relaxes me, except for those times it put me in the hospital. Gardening is about as relaxing as anything I know—so I don't understand why people have to make it competitive. They have big shows where they select the best rose. The best rose? Maybe somebody can explain to me what does a bad rose look like?

When I was growing up, my dad always had a garden in our backyard. Gary's and my job was to get the garden ready for planting in the spring. That was hard work, and just to make certain it stayed hard work as we got bigger, so did that garden.

There is something extraordinarily satisfying about growing your own beauty. I never have become bored of planting seeds in the ground and seeing flowers bloom. Not too many men like gardening when they're young. Men are in a hurry. That's our nature. And there is no such thing as speed gardening. But if there was such a thing as flower racing I'm sure it would be broadcast on ESPN. And people would be betting on it: Gimme the gardenia and three branches. But no matter what you do, you can't make flowers grow faster.

As men get older and slow down, we start appreciating things we've previously overlooked. It's a known fact that your taste buds change as you get older, so why shouldn't your taste? I loved working in my garden. But I can't garden anymore, I can't bend over to plant because my back goes into spasms. If I do it I'm going to mess up my back and be in bed for a week. And how do you explain to a doctor, I was just minding my own business when this petunia came along . . .

I know a lot about flowers. Plants too. I probably could have done the preshow show for the big gardening shows:

Ladies and gentlemen, I have never seen a more disgraceful performance than the azaleas'. They just plain wilted under the pressure.

Most of us work pretty hard, so we owe it to ourselves to find time for those things that give us real pleasure in life. Pleasure is payment for our hard work. It really is as simple as that.

CHAPTER 9

GOOD HEALTH DOESN'T HURT

MY MOMMA DID NOT WANT ME TO PLAY FOOTBALL. OH, Terry, she said to me when I started playing, it's too dangerous. You're the only son I've got besides your two brothers. Suppose you got hurt. Suppose little Mikey Ditka got mad at you and tried to rip out your lungs. Who would help your brother weed the garden?

She wanted me to play the piano. That's what she said. Except that every time I sat down to play the piano she'd scream at me, Terry Bradshaw, you stop banging on that piano right now if you know what's good for you.

Truth be told, we disagreed on what was good for me. I thought it was playing football. She was thinking more in terms of my father's belt across my backside. My mother really was afraid I'd get hurt. She didn't know anything at all about football except it was rough. But as my father convinced her, I didn't have to play football to get hurt. I had a natural talent for that.

My whole life I've always been able to find unique ways of getting hurt. It's one of my areas of expertise. Besides football, I've gotten hurt playing golf, I've gotten hurt cooking, I even got hurt in the Boy Scouts. Who knew the Boy Scouts was so dangerous? When my family moved from Shreveport to a small Iowa town my brother and I joined the Boy Scouts. This was one tough troop. Instead of merit badges they gave purple hearts. But they did not like new people, particularly new people who spoke with a Louisiana accent, so they were constantly making fun of us. After a scout meeting in the church one day I got in a fight with two of them. I was doing okay for a while, meaning basically I was surviving, when one of them grabbed my arm and swung me right through a plate glass door.

My mother didn't know what to be the most angry about: me getting in a fight at a Boy Scout meeting, me smashing the front door of the church, or having to take me to the doctor's office again to get stitches. My father got so mad at me for getting hurt that he gave me a whupping. I still might be the only person ever thrown out of the Boy Scouts—directly through a glass door.

I have been a very fortunate person. Except for eleven operations, four concussions that I know of, at least two broken noses, a broken thumb and broken collarbone, some shoulder separations, torn ligaments, broken little things in my neck that prevent me from turning ear to ear, herniated vertebrae in my back, some lost teeth, and getting more stitches than a baseball, I am in pretty good health. On a daily basis nothing really hurts me very much, unless you need to count breathing and moving. And I'm actually considered a player who got out of football without any serious injuries. Trust me, friends, the question you never want to ask at a pro football team reunion is How you feeling?

Sometimes I think the only part of a hospital in which I

haven't been a patient is the maternity ward. One time the doctor even suggested that instead of giving me stitches he put in a zipper.

So I appreciate the contribution good health makes toward leading a happy, fulfilling life. If you don't have good health, what do you have?

The answer is bad health. This is not a trick question. Am I going too fast for you?

The fact is that at least once in a while everybody has health problems. Everybody gets injured, some Terrys more than others. Everybody gets hurt or sick. Everybody. Pretty much the only way you can avoid health problems is by being dead. So the test is how we deal with them. Obviously I'm not talking about crippling injuries or serious illnesses, the kind of medical problems that require full attention. I'm talking about the things that happen to each of us every single day that generally don't involve linebackers.

I played football for about twenty years. My body took a tremendous pounding. But with the exception of the injury that forced me to retire, I probably didn't miss more than a dozen games because of injury throughout my entire career. And I never, truly never, missed a single game because of illness. I never missed a football game because I had the flu or a headache or a fever or a cold. No matter what was going on in my life, no matter how I was feeling, I showed up.

The first rule of success in anything you do is simply— show up. Be there, preferably on time, and prepared. Even when you don't feel like it. Just like everybody else, there were times during my football career when I didn't feel like going to work. When we had to go and play in Cleveland, for example, in the old stadium, that was not something I really looked forward to. Those Browns fans were tough. I mean, tough. They booed everything; they booed our bus driver so bad that poor man had to hang up his gearshift. And at times we had to play in the frigid cold. In Buffalo, Chicago, Cincinnati, and Pittsburgh. It got cold in Pittsburgh. Hey, I'm a Southern boy; if I stood in front of the ice box too long I started shivering. But I always showed up.

When I became a public speaker I made a commitment to be there. Fortunately, though, public speaking is an indoor sport. I've made several hundred speeches in my life. I've traveled when my back was hurting me so bad I could barely walk. I've traveled when I've had colds and the flu. I've traveled in good weather and bad weather. I showed up. One time, I remember, I was in Atlanta on my way to New York and a hurricane was moving up the east coast. A hurricane. I called my speaking agent, the Washington Speaker's Bureau, and I explained quite calmly that a hurricane was approaching and perhaps it might not be the best course of action for me to board an airplane about to take off.

What I really meant to say was, Do you believe I'm out of my $%$#@# mind? Do you honestly think there is the slightest ^%$%$#@ chance that I'm going to get on an airplane and fly into a hurricane?

It was calmly explained to me that my contract stipulated that if the plane took off, I had to be on it. I take my commitments seriously. I warned them that if my plane crashed I would never let them forget it. And then I got on the airplane. I showed up.

In fact, I've only missed one speech in my entire career. And

I am not afraid to put the blame for that directly where it belongs—on one of my ex-wives. She gave me the wrong date. The day I was supposed to be speaking to three thousand people in San Francisco I was in Denver, Colorado. She called me in a panic to tell me these people were waiting to hear me speak.

I expect they probably would not have appreciated what I said at that moment.

I got on the phone with these people and told them the truth. This was my fault, I said, I made a big mistake. I trusted my wife.

They were furious with me. They were livid. They told me I was the worst human being ever to set foot on this earth. They promised they would make me pay for this insult. They warned me that their lawyers—I offered to speak to this company the following year for free—were going to make me pay—"Free? Did that boy say, free?" The following year I flew to Toronto and spoke to this company for free. I showed up. It might have been a year late, but I showed up.

Health and fitness have always been an important part of my life as an athlete. I found the real secret of good health when I was young. That was it, being young. Nothing beats youth and good genes for good health. I really did get hurt a lot during my childhood, that being the result of the unique combination of my love for football, my undiagnosed Attention Deficit Disorder, and a general lack of good sense. I definitely got a lot of practice healing. I didn't need any formal exercise program because I was always moving. About the most I did was run to build up my stamina and lift weights to bulk up for football.

The first time I ever knew I had a medical problem was

when I took my draft physical. This was during the Vietnam era and I was ordered to report for my predraft physical. I wasn't Hall-of-Famer, four-time Super Bowl–champion Terry Bradshaw back then; I was just plain Bradshaw, Terry, another player on a small college football team. While I'll never know for certain, I suspect there was only one reason I didn't get drafted: absolute fear.

By the time I took my army physical all my banged-up and broken parts had healed. There was no reason I shouldn't have passed it. But after the doctor finished his examination he asked me, "How can a young, healthy college student have high blood pressure?"

I took a guess: Maybe because you're trying to send me to Vietnam where they're shooting at people. But truthfully this was surprising to me. In school the physical had been one of the few things I always passed. I had never had any real medical problems before. The closest I'd come to 4-F was second semester in seventh grade when they'd started teaching algebra. So the army doctors put me on medication and six weeks later I took the test again. This time they put me in a stone-cold room by myself, turned on all the lights, and made me sit on a table for a long time. As I sat there all I could think of was that my entire future life was about to be determined, that if I passed this physical I was probably going directly to Vietnam. The longer I waited the more time my fears had to build. By the time that doctor examined me my blood pressure was even higher than it had been the first time.

I was recalled for a physical six months later, but by then the selective service had instituted a number system and I drew a high number.

I didn't have any problem passing the physical when I was drafted by the Steelers, but then again, the only place they intended to send me was Pittsburgh. Health and exercise are major issues in pro football. Pro football teams have several doctors and trainers and exercise coaches. While few players are ever completely healthy after the first few games, the trainers will do whatever is necessary to get you ready to play: Oh, don't worry about it, Terry, it's only a separated head. We'll just glue it back on and you'll be ready to go Sunday.

Thanks, Doc. Hey, you didn't happen to find my knee lying around here somewhere, did you?

In pro football you just learn to live with pain during the season. During my career we didn't know as much about the effects of stimulants, "greenies" we called them, and steroids as we do now. I don't believe anybody realized how dangerous they were. People used stimulants to get way up for the game. Steroids were used to build muscle. There has been a lot of publicity about the use of pills but, truthfully, I never saw anyone using steroids. I'm not saying football players didn't use them, just that I never saw it. In fact, only once during my career did anyone even offer me a greenie. I didn't like stimulants. It wasn't our trainer, it was a kicker trying to make the team. We were in the locker room when he held out a little bag of pills and offered me one. A kicker! That was ridiculous. I didn't understand that. Why in the world would a kicker possibly need a stimulant? To keep him awake until he was needed?

It isn't a secret that all professional sports have had drug problems. Which probably puts them in the same category as just about every business. Truthfully, though, I'd rather that kicker be using drugs than the guy who fixed the brakes on my car. I've never used recreational drugs. I don't even like taking Ritalin for my ADD. What I just couldn't understand is why someone would work their whole life to reach the NFL or the NBA or the major leagues or even Roller Derby, and then just destroy their career. I didn't get it. To me that was just ridiculous. But I also resented what one person's drug use did to the team. Just one person using drugs can cause tremendous damage to a team, a family, or a business. Think of it this way: If my offensive lineman is using drugs and he misses a block I'm the one who's going to suffer because of it. If you've got a receptionist in your office using drugs, the whole office suffers.

My playing career was ended by an injury to my arm. I had an operation and tried to come back to play too soon. I believe if I would have taken more time to heal I probably would have been able to play again. But I know that if I had taken more time I wouldn't have been me. That's who I am. As my third ex-wife once said when asked about a television appearance I was about to make, "Terry is just going to be himself. That's what scares me."

After spending my childhood wanting only to play pro football, then spending the rest of my life playing pro football, I didn't know how not to play football. I wasn't prepared for a lot of things, but high among them was the fact that I was going to gain weight. I had never had a weight problem in my life. Former players had warned me that when I retired I was going to have to watch my weight. And I did, I watched it go right up. I didn't have the slightest idea how to lose weight. It was something I'd never had to worry about.

As a professional athlete, in fact, I really didn't even need to work out very much. To get ready for training camp I ran about four miles a day and then some sprints. That was pretty much it. I didn't have to exercise; with all the work we did in training camp and practice throughout the season I just never gained weight.

My normal playing weight was about 218, but one year I decided to report to training camp really light. I thought it might increase my mobility. So for a month before camp began the only thing I ate was tuna fish and crackers. Tuna fish and crackers for breakfast, for lunch, and for dinner. Sometimes if I got hungry I'd have a tuna fish snack. The real key to that diet, of course, is that you really, really have to like tuna fish. I reported to camp at 202 pounds. Oh, my goodness, I was beautiful. I have never looked so trim in my life. I swear, I wanted to have my mirror bronzed.

It was great until we started running sprints. That was when I passed out. I just didn't have any strength. So I started devouring carbs. I carbed up, way up. There is something very rewarding about having to eat french fries for your health.

But when I retired I started gaining weight. I got up as high as 248. I could hardly look at myself in the mirror. It seemed like every part of my body had gotten fatter—except my hair. My hair just kept getting thinner and thinner. In the years since I've retired I've tried just about every diet imaginable. I'd watch those late-night infomercials, in which a beautiful woman is admiring this guy with a six-pack while the announcer promises, "You too can look like this." And I'd think, the only way I could possibly look like that is to go out and get a DNA transplant.

I've probably tried twenty different diets. I've been on

them all. I've been on an all-protein diet. I've been on an all-salad diet. Nothing but salad and eggs. Part of my difficulty has always been my impatience; I need immediate results. If I start a diet in the morning, I expect to see results by late afternoon. The most effective diet I've ever been on was what I call my divorce diet. Every single time I was going through a divorce I lost weight. And I kept it off. That particular diet is very expensive though; considering what my divorces cost me it comes to several thousands of dollars a pound.

The best diet I've tried is the Slim Fast, and the Slim Fast people are not paying me to say that. Of course, if they'd like to, I'm very available. Now that diet doesn't work for everybody. I have a close friend who tried it and gained twenty pounds. I asked him, how in the world can you gain weight on Slim Fast?

"Well," he told me, "I really didn't like the way it tasted so I mixed it with ice cream."

But the best diet for someone like me, a person who doesn't have real good discipline, is a combination of fewer calories and a daily workout. It isn't any big secret; when I eat a little less and work out for forty-five minutes to an hour every day I don't have a weight problem. That's the one diet you never see advertised late at night on television because there's nothing to sell. Eat less, exercise, lose weight. Man, it couldn't be any simpler than that.

Before I hurt my back I was a runner. A jogger. I loved running. During my football career I only ran as a means of survival. But after I retired I started running for exercise. I ran six days a week, four miles each day. That was my distance, I was a four-miler. There were few things I enjoyed more than just going out running on back roads or through fields. Running for me was exercise for both my body and my mind. It enabled me to get rid of calories and stress. And running is easy, you don't even have to take lessons. You just keep putting one foot in front of the other as fast as you can—and you're running. There's no right or wrong way to run, nobody keeping score, you don't need to buy any expensive equipment.

When I was in shape I didn't even have to think about the fact I was running; my body knew how to do that, allowing my mind to go wherever it needed to. When I was running I would think about the things that needed to be done, or problems that had to be solved. Or maybe I would work on a speech I had to give, or decisions that had to be made. Sometimes I would think about the mistakes that I'd made—but that usually required more than a four-mile run. Running allowed me to release stress, to relax. And when I was done I felt just great—not because I had finished running but rather because I felt refreshed. Cleansed. I never felt the need to run a marathon; even I haven't made that many mistakes.

The only real health problem I've had that wasn't caused by playing football is my ADD. As I've written previously, it wasn't diagnosed until the early 1990's, when I decided to find out why I was so impulsive, why I had so much trouble just relaxing, why I was so—me.

School just wasn't fun for me. My first day in first grade, the first day, I got whacked. The teacher told us not to rock back and forth in our chairs. To which I naturally responded, you mean like this? And I didn't just rock back and forth, I actually fell over backwards. That teacher called me up to the front of the classroom and told me to turn over my hand. I wondered why she wanted me to turn over my hand. A piece of candy perhaps, for being so clever? Instead she took a ruler and smack!

Whack! I got that lesson real fast: School hurts.

Just think about it, I'll bet all of you have had a little Terry in your classroom. I was a nice person, I had a lot of friends, I never tried to cause problems, but I just couldn't stay still.

My ADD made learning difficult. No one had ever heard of Attention Deficit Disorder. There was no treatment, no medicines, and no special ed classes. I have what is now called an "auditory processing disorder." Back then it was just "Please sit down and be quiet, Terry. Don't make me tell you again." I was always nervous, always fidgety; I used to pull out my hair. I bit my fingernails right down to the second knuckle. I couldn't sit still and study. I couldn't get through a test. Reading was not a problem for me, I could always read; my problem was retaining what I had read. By the time I got to the middle of a paragraph I would forget what was at the beginning. It didn't even occur to me that there was something physically wrong with me; I just believed I was one of those people who had a hard time learning. Many of my teachers tried hard to help me, but they hadn't been trained to deal with this.

Playing football wasn't just something I enjoyed, it was absolutely necessary for me. It was the only outlet I had for all the energy trapped inside me.

Times have changed. The most important thing parents can do if they think their child has a learning disability or is hyperactive is get that child tested as early as possible and get that child the proper treatment if it is needed. People don't like to talk about things like this; no one wants to admit that their child is less than perfect. But listen to me, this is something parents really need to do.

I was surprised how many parents came up to me after reading *It's Only a Game* to tell me how much they appreciated the fact that I admitted I had ADD. They said they showed the book to their son or daughter and told them that if Terry Bradshaw could be successful, they could make it too. Because that Bradshaw definitely had a major case. I had this one mother come up to me, the poor woman was crying, the tears running out of her eyes, and she told me that her son had grown up with ADD and she hadn't known it, that she had thought he was just wild, just uncontrollable, and she was sorry for telling him he would never amount to anything.

"It's okay, Ma," I said, "don't worry about it."

ADD has affected my entire life. It caused a crack in my foundation. As a result I'm what would be politely called, unpredictable. ADD isn't something you get rid of; you just learn to cope with it. I've learned how to take responsibility for my actions. And I really do always show up on time and prepared. I take Aderol on a semiregular basis. I don't like to stay on any medication for too long, so every few months I'll go off it for a while and then go back on. People can usually tell when I'm not taking it because I'll do little things like sell the ranch, get divorced, even play golf without cheating.

I still have never learned how to relax. To just sit still. On a typical morning I've got to be going over to the barn and talking to everybody for a few minutes then coming back to the house and then going back to the other barn and hanging around there for a few minutes and then come back to the house and then go out and check on a horse and come back again and maybe fish for a half hour and come back into the house and smoke a cigar and go back over to the barn . . .

With all the injuries I've had, with the ADD, I have never spent one single minute feeling the slightest bit sorry for myself. I've been sad and I've definitely been depressed; I've sung the country songs, but I never asked for sympathy. I understand that compared to some other people my medical problems are minor. But I've also learned that other than your loved ones, people don't want to know about your problems. They've got their own problems and only a limited amount of worry time. They don't care if my back is killing me, or if I have serious personal problems. People just want you to do what you're supposed to do, to be where you're supposed to be when you're supposed to be there: Now, Terry, maybe you're not feeling so well, but you were supposed to be on my television set Sunday afternoon. I was needing a laugh and you weren't there.

Sorry, but I was dying.

Well, gosh, Terry, don't you go dying on Sunday afternoon. You got an obligation. Go die on your own time.

I found out a long time ago how other people would react if I really got sick and, my friends, it was not pretty. In 1988, while I was flying to Miami to give a speech to a refrigerator company I suddenly felt serious pains in my chest. I'd never felt anything quite like it, and that was awfully late in my life to be experiencing new pains. This isn't good, I thought. Actually, what I thought was, Oooo, thiss . . . oww . . . not good. I made my speech and by the time I finished I was drenched in sweat. Perspiration was dripping down my face, beads of sweat were dropping off my chin and my earlobes. Dang, those people must have thought, that Bradshaw certainly does get emotional about refrigerators.

I was pretty certain I was having a heart attack. I was forty years old and my heart was failing. Oh, I thought, please, anything but a heart attack. I went right to the hospital for tests. After a complete examination the doctors assured me that my heart was fine. I was relieved. But the reporters found out that I had been in the hospital. They wanted to know what was wrong with me. I didn't want to comment on it. What was I going to say, the hospital was having a sale on spleens? Finally I told reporters my problems were caused by fatigue. I had just been working too hard.

The pain didn't go away, though, which made me real nervous. After more tests the doctors told me they had found a spot on my chest X ray and they couldn't tell what it was. It could be anything from scar tissue to a tumor behind my heart. A tumor? Soon as I heard that I started wishing it was just a heart attack.

I didn't want to tell anybody. I didn't want anybody else worrying about me; I was doing enough worrying for everybody. But a TV station I worked for in Pittsburgh made it the lead story on their Saturday night newscast. Hold the cameras! Bradshaw might have a tumor! The Associated Press reported it and newspapers around the country carried the story. Somewhere the "might have" got lost. By Sunday afternoon I was practically dead. At least on paper. Bob Costas ended NBC's pregame show with the "sad" news, but added that everyone was praying for me. NBC was praying for me? Man, I had to be sicker than even I knew. When Bob Costas pronounces you dying, there is no sense fighting it.

Oh, man, did my phone start ringing. My momma called up crying, furious at me that I didn't tell her I was dying. Friends began planning my funeral. But I'm not dying, I told them. We love you, T, they said, you want us to play country music? Charla was very supportive; she was really worried about me.

On Monday the doctors told me the spot, and the pain, were being caused by scar tissue left from an injury I'd suffered in a softball game decades earlier. Hallelujah! I was going to live! Praised be! I was going to live!

Except on television. The man who originally reported the story insisted that he had a very good source for his story, and that he "would sort of expect Bradshaw to deny it." Hello? Of course I was going to deny it, it wasn't true. What else could I do? The doctors finally issued a press release stating that I had some scar tissue and that my condition was "not serious."

The phone stopped ringing. My friends canceled my funeral. And Charla? As I told one reporter truthfully, "It's funny how when you're going to be alive they don't care. They go shopping."

I suppose I'm like most people, I don't do everything that I should to maintain my health. For example, I've read that most studies seem to show that one glass of wine a day is good for your heart. Well, assuming that's true, at the rate of one glass a day I'm already safe till sometime in June 2088. Okay, I have been known to have a drink with friends. And strangers. I never did drink when I was playing, so I had some catching up to do. I don't know too much about wines; generally, if it doesn't have a screw top or come in a brown paper bag I'll drink it. I don't know regions or vines or which side of the slope the grapes came from. About all I do know is the two basic wine groups: red and white.

As far as good health is concerned, one thing I don't like at all is second-hand smoke. Not at all. I like my smoke first-hand. I have smoked cigars my whole adult life. My pawpaw chewed tobacco. My dad smoked cigars, King Edwards, and I just loved the aroma that filled the house. Maybe there is some deep psychological reason for it, or maybe it just smelled great. I started smoking cigars—*ceegars,* as we say in Louisiana—when I was at college. Smoking a cigar helped me study. Someone told me that the oral fixation helped me concentrate better. Maybe. But maybe it was also the fact that when I smoked my cigar everybody else left the room so the only thing I had to do was study. In Pittsburgh Mr. Rooney gave me all my cigars. I also chewed tobacco back then; I even did TV commercials for Red Man.

I've heard all the arguments against smoking. Believe me, I've heard them—pretty loudly. When I was married to my third ex-wife she tried hard to get me to quit. She complained about the smell in the house. So to satisfy her I did the manly thing: When I smoked a cigar I lit aroma candles, opened the windows, and turned on the fan.

I lead a semihealthy life. Maybe I drink a little and smoke a little and I pretty much eat what I feel like eating. The one thing I know that all the studies have shown is that the single most important thing a person can do for their health is exercise. I'm limited as to what I can do because of football injuries, but operation by operation I'm getting those things fixed. I love running and if I can't run I walk. Right at the beginning of this book I told you to pay no attention to what I say. With one exception: You want to be healthy, exercise. It doesn't matter what kind of exercise you do. Just exercise. Get your heart pumping. It's that simple.

There is one health-related question I do get asked more than any other. Parents ask me if they should let their sons play football. I am so glad I never had a son. In addition to the pressure that he would just naturally face being my son, if he wanted to play football he would continually be compared to me. Naturally I would never push him to play football, naturally. But the answer to that question depends on the age of the child. I just don't believe kids should play organized tackle football until their joints have closed, which is usually about thirteen years old. There is so much peer pressure on kids to play football before that age, and I don't believe they are ready for it. Too many young kids play football and get hurt and scared and lose interest in the game.

I think kids should be left alone to be kids. Let them do the same things my brother and I did when we were growing up. Except, maybe, for the unfortunate baseball bat episode and getting thrown through the church door.

CHAPTER 10

You Are Your Most Important Product

I WAS ALMOST FIFTY YEARS OLD WHEN MY THIRD marriage ended. I didn't know anything about dating. I definitely did not know how to go about meeting women. The fact is I was hurting emotionally too deeply to be much good to anybody, but I needed companionship. I was available. I was definitely available. I wanted someone to have fun with, but I had absolutely no idea how to meet women. I could have gone to my church but my church is very small and I already knew everybody. So every time I went out of the house my eyes were wide open. When I went to the grocery store, for example, I'd check out everybody there; but it's hard to meet a nice available woman in the frozen foods.

By my own self I wasn't doing very well at meeting people at all. But many of my friends offered to introduce me to people. I went on several blind dates. Although these were nice women, generally there was no chemistry. Going on blind dates is like throwing a pass; most of them are either going to be incomplete or go for a short gain. Once in awhile you're going to get slammed really hard—but on occasion you're going to complete one for a touchdown.

I did keep trying. Oh, Lord, I did keep trying. Finally, one evening I picked up my blind date and, oh, my goodness gracious, this was one beautiful woman. This was it. This was the one. She was pretty and smart and nice and best of all, she was with me. We drove to dinner at a lovely restaurant and we seemed to be getting along very well. Sometimes it just happens. We laughed for most of the night. About halfway through dinner I just happened to notice that her left hand had edged just a bit closer to my right hand. Just a couple inches. If we had been married I wouldn't have even noticed, but this being our first date I figured that probably meant she wanted to marry me and have my children and we would happily spend the rest of our lives together. So gently, sweetly, I put my right hand on top of her hand to hold it.

She jerked it away. That was a message; the message was don't you go touching my hand. It was kind of embarrassing, so I said, "I'm sorry, I didn't mean to offend you."

"Terry," she admitted, "there's no tingle."

I said, "There's no tingle?"

"That's right, there's no tingle."

In one split second we had gone all the way from happy-ever-after to no tingle. It was hard to accept. I knew I wasn't the best-looking guy in the world, I knew that because every Sunday during football season I sit next to Howie Long, who does happen to be the best-looking guy in the world, but I definitely thought I had at least a little tingle. "Define tingle," I said.

The woman did not even hesitate long enough to make me

think she might have had trouble with her answer. "I swore to myself that I would never date anybody who wasn't Catholic," she began, "and you're Baptist. I swore that I would never date anyone ten years older than me and you're twenty years older than I am. I promised myself I would never date anyone who's divorced and you've been divorced at least twice that I know of. I promised myself I would never date anyone who has kids and you have two of them." Finally, she paused, and I thought she was finished. She wasn't, she was just working up to the big time. "And you're bald."

Now that is the definition of no tingle. "Well, lemme just ask you then," I replied, "exactly why did you go out with me on this date, because you already knew all these things?"

"Oh, I just wanted to know what it was like to be out with a celebrity."

"I hope you enjoyed it," I said, "because it's over."

As we all get reminded on occasion, rejection is part of life. A big part of my life. Most people know about my high-profile success in football, but in my life I have been rejected, criticized, booed, brushed off, jeered, and replaced; I've been canceled, cut, benched, remaindered, ridiculed, and released. If you can think of another word for failure, I've been that too.

But I kept trying. I never quit. No matter what people said, I still recorded another record, I made another TV show, I appeared in another movie. What I am, I've discovered, what we all are, are salespeople. I'm a salesman and my product is myself. That's what I'm offering when I speak or when I appear on television. There are a lot of people who sell merchandise for a living—I've done that too—but everybody has to sell themselves. We are all selling all the time. And the techniques

179

of selling, whatever the product, are pretty much the same.

Almost everything we do in life involves selling. When I went into the huddle with my team I had to sell the play we were running. I had to make them believe this was the best possible play in that situation, that this was the very play that the Lord himself had sent down. When I do a commercial I have to convince the viewers that my product somehow will make their lives better. On *NFL Sunday* my job is to sell my personality so viewers will want to watch our show. When I'm with my kids I'm selling them the fact that my advice is worth following. When I go out on a date I'm selling myself, although sometimes, as I've described, the result is my date goes for the double-your-money-back offer. When I'm speaking I'm selling myself and my few simple ideas.

You're selling too. At your place of business, for example, you're selling competence, personality, dedication to both your fellow workers and your customers or clients. When you men asked that pretty woman to marry you, you got down on your hands and knees and you got after it. I mean, you sold: Sharon Jean, I'm telling you that I have never met anyone in my whole entire life as good as you. Girl, I can't live another day without you. I want you to be my wife. I can't live without you. I want you so bad, you fine little thing you. My life won't be complete if I have to go one more day without you being part of it. I don't want to breathe the air if you aren't by my side. I have never felt this way about anything in my life and I know I never will again. I love you so very much my darlin', there is no one like you in the whole wide world and no matter how long I live, you are the one and the only person for me.

I gave that speech three times.

But when you gave that speech you were selling yourself. You sold the best product you have. You were amazing.

And you women, you invested in your product, in yourself. You went out and you bought the prettiest dress you could find, and the prettiest shoes and you spent seven hours in front of the makeup mirror perfecting that casual look. And you did it because you realized that you were a salesperson and you wanted to market the best possible you.

In preparation for my speeches I've read a lot of the motivational books, and the books written by Og Mandino, particularly *The World's Greatest Salesman*, have always made the most sense to me. He pretty much summed up my personal sales technique when he wrote, "If you bring joy, enthusiasm, brightness and laughter to your customers, they will react with joy, enthusiasm, brightness and laughter and your weather will produce a harvest of sales and a granary of gold for you."

I call that technique, being me. For whatever reasons, my natural instinct is to try to make people happy. As I've explained, I automatically want to be nice, I like making people smile. And I have been blessed with the ability to talk and say funny things. Obviously not in this particular paragraph, but in my life. Humor has always come easy for me.

When I pick up the telephone to make a call, for example, someone comes over me. And I never know who that someone is going to be until I open my mouth and that character comes out. My mother is my best target. I'll call her and in a strange voice tell her, "Mrs. Bradshaw? This is Clyde C. Johnson, C. C. Johnson's Exterminating Service down here in Texas. I'm 'fraid I got to give you sad news, ma'am. Seems like your son,

Mr. Terry Bradshaw, well, apparently he was having a problem with Texas Giant rodents on his ranch. Seems like they were attacking his horses—I got to tell you I been in this bizness twenty-eight years, Mrs. Bradshaw, and I tell you the truth, I never in my life have seen such big rodents. I mean, they were standing up on their legs and picking the apples off his tree. So we laid out those giant rat traps that we got, you know, the five-footers with the steel snapper bars, and Mr. Bradshaw came home last night in the dark and—Mrs. Bradshaw, it says here you and Mr. B. Bradshaw are his next of kin, am I correct about that?"

I've definitely got my mother confused. One time she had a real call from the vice president of a credit card company who wanted to find out if someone had stolen my father's card number. He began by explaining the situation, telling her that an unusually large sum of money had been charged to the card, but she interrupted and said, "Terry, how are you?"

The banker was confused. "I'm sorry."

"I know it's you, Terry. You're not going to fool me again. I'm getting a little too smart for you."

After failing to convince my mother that he actually was calling from the bank, he asked, "Um, Mrs. Bradshaw, is your husband at home?"

"No," she said triumphantly, "your dad's not here."

I don't think we got that problem straightened out until I called a day or so later and my mother told me confidently, "You know, Terry, nobody's ever gonna believe you're a banker."

Obviously, not everybody is going to think I'm funny. I've always figured that of all the people watching *NFL Sunday,* or sitting in the audience when I give a speech, about half the people will enjoy what I have to say and the other half won't like me. There are people who think I'm loud, ill-informed, and silly. Mostly, those are the people I try not to date.

There isn't a salesman in the world who has closed every sale. It took me quite a while to accept the fact that there were people who weren't going to like me—even if I told them my joke about the careless butcher who got a little behind in his work. And that sometimes it didn't matter. That sometimes all that matters was the quality of my work.

Success happened very fast for me. One year I was the second-string quarterback at Louisiana Tech in Ruston, Louisiana, two years later I was the number one draft choice in the National Football League. In college we rarely played in front of more than ten thousand people. Just to give you some idea of the value of a college education, only two years after graduating I was in Pittsburgh being booed by seventy thousand people.

There is nothing that can prepare you for that. It was humiliating. I'd never been booed in high school or college. Shreveport was such a friendly place even our ghosts wouldn't boo. Most people go their entire lifetime without ever getting booed. I mean, just imagine what it would be like to have people stand around you while you're doing your job booing and screaming insults at you: You call that using a computer? Get a pencil, you bum! Or, Hey, Doc. You couldn't fill that cavity with a backhoe! Or, You're the worst teacher in the world! You couldn't teach a mosquito bite to itch!

At first I was devastated. At second and third too. Those people didn't care if I was a nice person. They weren't interested in my sense of humor. All they cared about was how well I did my job. I guess it was not surprising that my sense of humor became so much better after we'd won our first Super Bowl. I also became better looking.

What did I do when I was the focus of Steelers fans' unhappiness? I worked harder. I studied harder. I practiced harder. When I got knocked down I got right back up, spit out my teeth, and went back to work. I admit that at times my confidence wavered. Sometimes it's hard to remain convinced that seventy thousand people are wrong and you're right, but I knew I had the ability to do my job. For me, the hardest thing was keeping my confidence through the tough times. There's no tingle? Gimme the opportunity, I'll tingle you.

Several years ago the Avis car rental people boasted in their advertising, "We're Number Two. We Try Harder." That campaign never did make a lot of sense to me. Why would a company brag about being second? Maybe for one year it might be all right to admit that, especially if you're coming from way down, but after that year the question I would ask is, why aren't you number one? Apparently you're not trying hard enough. I think I'll take my business to number one.

If you'd like to lose your money, I have a good suggestion for you. At just about every sports event you see people hoisting a sign showing a hand with the index finger raised—meaning we are number one. My suggestion is that you make a similar sign, but instead of one finger, have two fingers raised. We're number two! Listen up, you make a sign like that, you'll be out of business in weeks. Because people don't want to be number two. They want to be the best that they can be.

In life, just as in business, it is impossible to overestimate the importance of self-confidence. If you don't believe in yourself, I'm definitely not going to believe in you. When I'm on an airplane I don't want to hear the pilot announce, I hope we're going to land in Los Angeles in two hours. I want to hear him boast, We're gonna be on the ground at LAX at exactly eighteen minutes after three o'clock!

I've never been satisfied being second at anything I've done. When I was working as a game analyst at CBS with Verne Lundquist, for example, we were the number-two broadcasting team behind John Madden and Pat Summerall; which is sort of like being runner-up to God and St. Peter, assuming St. Peter was doing the play-by-play. Being number two bothered me so much I decided to quit. As it turned out I didn't have to, as CBS put me in the studio for its pregame program.

I guess I felt that way because I come from a very competitive family. My little brother Craig, for example, was never happy being the youngest of three brothers. He's been trying his whole life to work his way up to middle brother. My older brother Gary and I were always in competition: Who can brush his teeth faster? Who can make Dad madder? Who can run faster away from Dad? Who can cry the loudest when Dad whomps you? Even today, when my family gets together we play games like Liverpool rummy or dominoes or rook and we're serious. My momma does not like to lose. She is the only person I've ever known who plays cutthroat dominoes. When she puts on that green plastic eyeshade and lights her cigar, don't nobody with a healthy survival instinct get in her way. And she was always the fastest tooth brusher in the family, although admittedly she had the advantage of only having that one tooth.

The person I've always competed hardest against is myself. My objective is to be the best possible Terry Bradshaw. When I chucked the javelin I was just trying to throw it farther than I'd thrown it the last time. If somebody could throw it farther than me, there wasn't too much I could do about it. Nobody plays defense in javelin chucking. For me, life is like golf; in golf you don't play against the other players, you play against the course. You don't try to stop other players—unless maybe you whup the flag—you win by taking the fewest swings at the ball. It really shouldn't matter how many refrigerators your competition sells, or how much money somebody else makes; it doesn't matter how much hair another man has on his head—what matters is how well you do. You are the only one who can make you better.

The only measuring stick worth using is your own. When I was growing up, about every six months my momma would make Gary and me stand against the door frame and draw a line to see how much we'd grown. Gary had his marks and I had mine. My momma was always careful to stand me up next to my own previous marks—because that was the only accurate measure of my progress. It'd make no sense for her to compare me with Gary's marks: Well, Terry, you've grown almost a foot and, Gary, sorry but you've lost five inches.

Business is like that too. Suppose one year I get real lucky and make 500 percent as much as I made the year before, and that same year Mr. Bill Gates has a terrible year and makes only 1 percent of what he'd earned the year before. If I was foolish enough to compare myself with Bill Gates it would seem like I had a terrible year, but measured against my own self I did just fine thank you very much but please don't tell the IRS. I promise you one thing; no matter how many sales you make, no matter how much money you earn, no matter how many hairs you grow on your head—somebody is going to do better. I guarantee it—although admittedly, when it comes to hair, that somebody is definitely not going to be me.

In everybody's life there are years when everything just seems to go perfectly; the bathroom pipes in your house don't get stuffed up once, the dry cleaner doesn't shrink a single thing, you sell more electric tummy tuckers than anybody in the entire eastern regional office, every stock you own goes up and your mortgage rates go down, you find out that your spouse's divorce lawyer goes to a dentist who owes you a big-time favor, the microwave breaks the day *before* your warranty expires, the people who invented business voicemail try to contact you and your answering machine keeps cutting them off—and you quarterback your football team to victory in the Super Bowl. It is the greatest year of your life, so great that Michael Eisner, the head of Disney, tells people that he's going to celebrate by going to your house! In fact, there is only one problem with all of that—you have to do it all again the next year.

When the Steelers won the Super Bowl for the first time in 1975 the city of Pittsburgh threw us a big parade. It was a wonderful celebration. I was riding in a nice convertible. I had been practicing my wave, I used that little wrist shake, and I was waving at people. How you doin'? Nice to see you! Everybody was cheering for us, holding up nice signs, throwing confetti. But as we rounded a corner I noticed one man standing all by himself. He had a megaphone. "Hey, Bradshaw!" he yelled at me. "You idiot. You'd better win that sucker again next year, boy, or we will run your butt out of this town." Winning one Super Bowl wasn't enough for him. That was down forever in the history books. That was finished. Now we had to prove it wasn't just a lucky year.

We are always measured against our best performance. That's why my momma always made me stand against the last mark she'd made for me. Once you've established a level of professionalism you're expected to do it again. To get better. There once was a baseball pitcher named Billy Loes who almost won twenty games one season. He wasn't disappointed when he didn't make it, telling reporters, "If I do it once, they'll just expect me to do it again."

But in 1976 we came back and did it again. We won our second consecutive Super Bowl. We were two-time Super Bowl champions! And they gave us another parade. Not many people get one parade, now we've got two. A bigger parade. The people were cheering even louder than the year before. They had bigger signs, they were throwing bigger confetti. It was incredible. I had my wave down pretty good, I was moving my entire arm and shaking my wrist. But as we turned a corner there was that same man from the year before. Still standing all by himself. He lifted up his megaphone and shouted at me, "Hey, Bradshaw, you dummy! You just better win that sucker again next year or we'll run your butt right outta town."

How tough is that? We'd won two consecutive Super Bowls. But that wasn't enough to satisfy this man. No siree. This was a real Pittsburgher. Tough, very tough. He didn't want to know what we'd already done, he wanted a commitment that we would do it again.

The only people interested in the past are history teachers.

The company you work for doesn't care how well you did last year; your boss wants to know how good you're going to do this year. Your patients don't care how many cavities you filled last year; their teeth are hurting right now. The people on your route don't care that you picked up one hundred tons of garbage last year, they've got new garbage that needs to be collected.

I'm not going to lie to you, least not in this sentence, it gets tougher to improve every year. After we'd won two consecutive Super Bowls every other team in the NFL was aiming at us. They wanted the prestige of beating us. That made it much tougher for us. The first year we'd sort of snuck up on the league. They didn't notice us getting a little better every year. They had been beating the Steelers for fifty years; nobody took us too seriously. Some teams were so confident they didn't even send the varsity. That second year it was tougher, but we had experience and confidence. But after we'd won our second championship the whole league knew how good and tough we were.

The next two years we did not win the Super Bowl and I didn't go anywhere near that corner. But we definitely heard it from the fans. We were still a fine football team, we won a lot of games, but we didn't win the Super Bowl. Nobody can be the champion every year. In 1978 we won fourteen games and lost only two. Was it a bad year because we didn't win another Super Bowl? We had a great season. We weren't the champions, but we still were a great team. No player on that team ever stopped trying. I believe if you stopped by Rocky Bleier's house today he'd be outside blocking for the mailman. As long as you can look yourself in the mirror without having to put on one of those plastic glasses and mustache disguises because you're embarrassed that you didn't do your best, you've had a good year.

We came back in 1979 to win our third Super Bowl. And we got another parade. This time I was sitting in a limousine and I was giving it the full-arm, wrist-twirl-side-to-side wave. You never heard such cheering. The signs were so big it took four people just to hold up one of them. The confetti was too big to throw, they were just rolling it at us. This was definitely the greatest celebration in Pittsburgh history since they discovered the first pit mine. But when we rounded that corner— there he was again. "Yo! Hillbilly! You dumb-head boy, look at me. Where you been at the last two years? I been standing here waiting for you. I'm telling you, you don't win that thing next year don't you come back here. We'll run you out on a boxcar, you hear!"

And the next season we won again. No team had ever won four Super Bowls. And Pittsburgh gave us the biggest parade yet. I had my own limousine and I was so important I had my own designated waver sitting next to me waving his arm for me. The signs were so huge people standing under them got frostbite because they blocked out the sun. The confetti was so big it took two people just to drop it in our path. But when we rounded that corner there he was again, just waiting for me. "Listen up, Bradshaw. That's enough, even if you don't win next year you can stay here!"

No, he definitely did not say that. He said the same thing he always said: "Listen up, Bradshaw, you sorry-assed brain drain. You think those four Super Bowl rings impress me! I'm telling you, if you don't win one for the thumb I personally am gonna march you outta this town and you ain't ever coming back."

Far as I know that man is still standing there. It seems to me he was just like a lot of people in this world, not including you and me, of course, but all those other people who choose to spend their lives waiting for the parade to come to them.

We won four Super Bowls because we were not the same team every year. Every year we changed a few parts, we got tuned up, we added a few new players and subtracted a few. We kept the same core team—twenty-two players participated in all four Super Bowl victories—but our offense and defense continued to change, it kept evolving. We were the same team but we were different. We had to change just to keep pace with our opponents. If you try to sell the same thing this year the same way you sold it last year you're not going to survive too long. There is a technical word used in business to describe people who don't keep up with their competitors, who don't continually change; and that word is *unemployed*.

I know change isn't easy, I know that. We all fall into comfortable patterns. When I was in England my difficulty in changing to meet new realities nearly got me killed. Every time I tried to cross the street I looked to my left, just as I would at home, and stepped off the cur— whoosshh! Cars came racing at me from my right. I couldn't get used to the fact that in England they drive on the opposite side of the street from America. It took me nearly a week before I could safely cross the street. And I wasn't the only person who had this problem. British people told me they suffer an extremely high number of head and shoulder injuries in the summer months—Americans who look the wrong way before crossing

191

the street keep landing on them: Ooooh, I say, old chap, watch out for those pesky flying Yanks!

Sometimes you just have to force yourself to change your habits. I lived to throw long passes, it was my passion. But when opponents covered my deep receivers I took what they left open; I threw those dinky little short passes and after the game I snuck out the back door of the stadium.

At the beginning of my broadcasting career CBS teamed me with Verne Lundquist. Verne was as smooth as silicon on silk, as easy as water running downhill. He would set the scene and allow me to step into it. He let me ramble, and ramble and . . .

But after two seasons CBS teamed me with Tim Ryan. Tim had a completely different style than Verne. He talked a lot more, so naturally I just kept quiet. Nobody knew what had happened to me. I was so quiet that my friends wanted to put my picture on a milk carton.

. . . ramble . . .

CBS Sports Executive Producer Ted Shaker was very honest about the fact that if I didn't change, if I didn't adapt to my new partner my new nickname would be "Remember," like in "Remember Terry Bradshaw?" It was tough for me to change. I was having a good time in the booth and I thought that as long as I had a good time viewers also would have fun. That's the way it had always worked on the golf course. But Ted Shaker pointed out that many of these people were watching the football game because they liked watching the football game. That it was time for me to stop being silly, that rather than trying to entertain viewers I was being paid to offer insightful analysis in an entertaining way. I think he might have said something like if he wanted a comedian he would have hired Dennis Miller.

To survive as a broadcaster I had to change my entire approach. I had to learn to control myself in the booth. I had to learn when to talk and when to be quiet. If you don't think that was hard for me, just ask my mother. For almost forty years she'd been pleading with me for that exact same thing: Terry! Control yourself! But CBS expected me to learn how to do it in a few months. The big difference, I think, was that my mother didn't pay nearly as well as CBS. And I knew my contract to be her son didn't expire.

I really had to work at it. If change was so easy beauty salons couldn't be charging women hundreds of dollars to change their hair color. For me, change was a big risk. Being good ole Terry had worked out pretty well; now they were telling me to take myself a little more seriously. So I spent time speaking with people in broadcasting whom I respected. I learned how to focus. I learned how to prepare for a game. Eventually I got really adequate. When I started taking myself a little more seriously, so did viewers. The fact is that people who refuse to adapt to the changes going on around them are one day gonna get badly hurt landing on some Englishman.

One other thing you are going to have to learn how to do in your business or personal life is negotiate. For example, the next time my contract is up with the fine, upstanding gentlefolk at Fox I intend to go firmly into the head office, maybe casually carrying my Emmy—I'll tell them I'm just dropping it off at the dry cleaners—and declare, "I want to be paid fifteen million dollars or I'm walking."

And then, while I'm taking that walk I'll decide that maybe

I could find a better way to negotiate. All right, I am probably not the best person to be giving advice about negotiating. During my playing career I never was represented by an agent. I always believed I was fairly paid; I was too; my pay was only fair while other quarterbacks who did not win four Super Bowls were being paid very, very well.

Now really, what chance did I have to negotiate a good contract for myself? I was negotiating with businessmen, people who negotiated several hundred contracts a year; that's what they did for a living. Their job description read: Pay Bradshaw as little as possible. I negotiated one contract every few years; my job description included throwing passes, handing off, and showing up. Psychologically I wasn't capable of being a tough negotiator. Just about the most important thing for me was to be liked and respected. As I found out, the less money people had to pay me the more they liked me. The Steelers loved me. And they respected the fact I really didn't know how to negotiate a contract.

Now suppose I had been a tough negotiator. Suppose I had demanded to be paid as much as the highest-paid quarterback in the league. Just suppose I had threatened to sit out the whole season if they didn't agree to my demands and suppose I had gone to the newspapers and complained about the way I was being treated; if I had done all that and managed to squeeze a few more dollars out of the Steelers would I have respected myself?

Well, of course I would have. Dang right. You bet. How can I ask myself a dumb question like that? The mistake that I made was I confused my financial value to the Steelers with my own emotional well-being. I sometimes forgot that I was selling a disposable product with a limited shelf life—me.

I've learned a lot since then. I've learned that my best ne-
gotiation skill is hiring someone who knows what he's doing,
someone who is not emotionally involved with my money: and
then get out of his way. My talent is that I make it seem like I
have no talent, and believe me, it takes a lot of talent to do
that.

Like everybody else, I'm a salesman. My product is myself.
My time. My reputation. My ability to entertain people. My
ability to attract attention. I always had confidence in myself,
I've just never been comfortable bragging about my accomplishments. I've never worn a Super Bowl ring. In fact, during
my career the closest I ever came to boasting was pointing out
to the Steelers one time, "You may not win with me, but you
definitely won't win without me."

That statement, by the way, was misquoted by former Gi-
ants quarterback Dave Brown, who told reporters after leading
New York to a win over the Saints, "I read one quote from
Terry Bradshaw that kind of motivated me. It said, 'You can
lose with me playing quarterback, but you can't win with me.'
It was something I kind of took to heart."

I can tell you how much I get to make a speech, how much
I charge to do a commercial, what those nice people at Fox pay
me to sit next to Howie and Mr. James Brown. And just like
me, you can put an economic value on your services and you
can put a price on your product. But also just like me you have
a hard time figuring out your own value.

Listen to me carefully now, 'cause I may not be right about
a lot of things but I know I'm right about this: Your value has
nothing to do with how much money you have in the bank or

the total amount of your investments; it isn't how much you earn every year—and if you think it is then you're wrong. You can't figure out your value from a bank book or a payroll stub—although, actually, I know three divorce lawyers who would be willing to try.

You're priceless. Me too. There's only one of each of us. We're special, unique. When they made you they broke the mold. Look, the value you have to your business is what those people are willing to pay you to do your job. And I'm positive you're worth it. But let me remind you of something; if you don't go to work one day the company is going to get along without you. After a few days they may even let somebody else sit in your chair. Only on the edge at first, but after a while they'll let him lean all the way back. A few weeks later that person is going to be using your coffee mug. Yes! They're letting someone else use your coffee mug! A month later that person is taking your place and making a fool of their very own self at the Christmas party.

Suppose my good friend Jeff Quinn worked for Microsoft for fifty years. Half a century. Jeff is such a dedicated person he definitely would have been showing up for work twenty years before they even founded the company. He would be there the day they opened the doors for business. In the whole fifty years he wouldn't miss one day of work. He'd even go to work on Saturdays. But when he retired nothing would change. They wouldn't change the name of the company to Microsoft Minus Jeff Quinn. It would be business as usual—although they probably wouldn't let anyone else use Jeff's mug. Out of respect.

Now just suppose you go missing from home for a day;

maybe not even a whole day, just a few hours. Your family is going to notice you're not there. They're going to miss you. They're not going to let anybody else sit in your chair. There's no, "Mom's not home today so we hired a temp to fill in." If you're not home for a week I promise you nobody is going to be using your mug. They're not going to let anybody else make a fool of themselves at the Christmas party; that's your job. Nobody is ever going to replace you; people who matter in your life, your family and friends, the people who depend on you for small kindnesses are going to miss you every day. Now how are you going to put a value on that?

CHAPTER 11

THE BEST THING IN LIFE IS LIFE

I WENT FOR A WILD RIDE WITH DALE EARNHARDT ONE
Saturday afternoon in February 2001. That is something I will
never forget. Never. When you grow up in the South you love
car racing. Not those fancy formula one cars; maybe you love
those cars if you grow up in the south of France. But souped-
up road cars, real stock cars, the direct descendants of the cars
moonshiners used to get away from revenuers.

In my growing-up days people raced hot rods for a few
bucks on back roads and dirt tracks. Now it's a billion-dollar
business; it's NASCAR and the races are held in huge stadiums. It's the most popular spectator sport in America. Dale
Earnhardt was the greatest driver in NASCAR history, and he
was a friend of mine.

When I started broadcasting for CBS in the 1980's in addition to football I was assigned to cover the Iditarod dog sled
race across Alaska as well as several NASCAR events. Maybe
CBS figured these races were so simple to broadcast that even
I couldn't mess up. I mean, there isn't too much strategy in
dog sled racing: It's pretty much, Run, Spot, Run. And an-

nouncing the actual race is pretty easy: They're off. Boy, it's cold.

NASCAR wasn't hard to broadcast either: Here they come, there they go. Here they come again, there they go again. But I loved doing it. I admired the drivers; they got to drive as fast as they could, as close to the next car as they dared; they could even run other drivers off the road. For doing exactly the same kind of things we get tickets for, they got a standing ovation: Oh, man, Clyde, you see how he cut that other guy off!

Dale Earnhardt was the king of the race track. We'd met several times. We just hit it off. There was a mutual respect between us. So when Fox suggested I do a piece with him at the Daytona International Speedway I loved the idea. It was like getting paid to go play with a friend. I took my girls with me and we went to Daytona Beach, Florida, where he was racing in the Daytona 500.

The night before the race he took me for a ride around the track. Going for a ride around the track with Dale Earnhardt is not like driving down to the store—unless you want to get to the store really, really fast. I swear, there was no space between the accelerator and the floorboard. We were probably going 140, maybe 150 miles an hour and Dale suddenly started getting upset. My friends, when someone is driving approximately 140 miles an hour you do not want them getting upset. You want them to be happy. I mean, happy! I asked him what was wrong.

They'd put a governor on the car, he told me, a device to restrict the speed. This was as fast as he could crank up that baby. Apparently it wasn't fast enough for him.

Oh, man, I said with as much disappointment as I could muster, that sure is too bad. Tsk, tsk. Right. Let me tell you something, if I could have met the person who put on that governor, I probably would have kissed him. I didn't need to go any faster. We weren't heading anywhere, we were just driving in a big circle around the track; I didn't care that much if it took an extra two, three seconds. I admit it, I was scared. It was not fun.

As we drove along Dale told me with real excitement in his voice how he would attack each turn on the track. He told me about the dip in turn four, for example. And he said, If I'm up high on turn two I'll need to get down quick—and then he just yanked the steering wheel and wewentdownquick. I don't think I'd had as much fun since I'd gone parasailing with my third ex-wife and the tow rope broke with us way up in the air.

Dale was having a great time, though. At one point he was explaining to me that at those speeds the slope of the track would actually hold the car in a groove. I didn't doubt him, not even for one little second did I doubt that was true, but he still wanted to prove it to me. So he let loose of the steering wheel and turned around to speak directly to the camera in the rear of the car. He was laughing.

Sometimes things don't instantly register on your brain. However, this wasn't one of those times. When he took his hands off that steering wheel I realized it immediately. But what could I say; Uh, excuse me, Dale, maybe you didn't notice but we are going one hundred and forty miles an hour and you seem to have taken your hands off the steering wheel? I just held on tight as possible and tried not to show my fear. It was one of those times when I reminded God how good I'd been lately.

It only lasted a few seconds, just long enough for me to be terrified. Then he drove us into the pits and spun the car. A doughnut. As he hopped out of the car he told me, "Hey, let's pretend we've won the race!" Far as I was concerned we had won. I was still in one piece. I'm a white boy, but I have never been whiter in my whole life than I was at that moment. So sure I was going to cheer. We leaped on the hood of the car and started jumping up and down.

I saw him again the next morning, the morning of the race. After hugging on my girls just a bit he grabbed the back of my neck and pulled me forehead to forehead and said to me, "I can't begin to tell you how happy I am to see you here. You're like my good luck charm. Every time you come down I drive well."

We couldn't stay till the end of the race. We had to leave early to beat the traffic. Otherwise it would have been at least three hours before our plane took off and I wouldn't have been able to get the girls back to their mother on time. When we left, Dale Earnhardt was running with the leaders, his usual place, with about twenty laps to go.

My phone was ringing when I got home. It was my brother Gary. "You hear?" he asked.

"Hear what?"

"Dale Earnhardt got killed on the last lap." I couldn't believe it. It just wasn't possible. I turned on the TV and watched him hit the wall going into turn three. And then I watched it again and again. I got sick to my stomach. It was just awful. Terrible. Over and over in my mind I saw him taking his hands off the wheel and turning to look at me and he's got that big happy grin on his face. I could hear him laughing. I can still hear the sound of his laughter.

I was probably in shock for three or four days. Then I got real depressed. Dale and I were almost the same age; it occurred to me that if it could happen to him it certainly could happen to me. That scared me. But if there is anything positive to be learned from his death it is that Dale Earnhardt died doing what he loved most of all in the world. He spent his last day on earth living his life to the fullest extent.

One of the most difficult things for all of us to do is squeeze as much pleasure out of every single day as we can manage. Forget about yesterday because there isn't too much you can do to change it and don't worry about tomorrow because by the time you get there the whole world will have changed. Live for today. There are no instant replays in life.

Every night when you get into bed and lay your head down on the pillow, pray that you can say to yourself, one good something happened to me today. Because if you can't say that, then you've wasted one whole day. And every day wasted is one less day you have. I guarantee that at the end of all your days you're going to wonder, why did I waste so much time? You just have to keep things simple: Appreciate what you have every day.

It just seems to me that too many people waste the present feeling sorry about yesterday and fretting about tomorrow. I try hard to live in the present, and often I succeed. I definitely have some regrets about the past and I have plans for the future, but I try to focus my energies on the present. I think there are few people with stronger connections to yesterday than retired professional athletes. For many of us that period was the best times of our lives. We were men getting paid to play a game we loved, our teams took good care of us, and people we didn't even know held us in great esteem. And if we choose to, we can continue to profit from our accomplishments in the past. Mining the past is a big-time industry. I can't even begin to estimate how many offers I've gotten to attend autograph shows or sign a certain number of jerseys or footballs to be sold, and I've turned down many more than I've accepted.

I really don't know what satisfaction people get from having the signature of a celebrity. It makes no sense to me, and I believe that even when I'm in my home looking at the autographs I got from Burt Reynolds and former secretary of defense William Cohen and Joe Montana.

Generally I don't mind signing autographs. If all it takes to make a person happy is my scrawl on a piece of paper or a handshake I'm pleased to be able to do it. I understand I have a responsibility. And you can read my signature, I don't just scrawl "T%^&^ Br$#@%." I write my name neatly and legibly. I do that because growing up I had a lot of practice writing. My specialty was "I will not talk in class. I will not talk in class."

Through the years I've found that most people are nice and polite when they ask for my autograph. Most people. Well, there was that Cowboys fan in Albuquerque, New Mexico, who came up to me while I was eating and stuck a gun in my ribs. I certainly handled that one well; I grabbed the barrel of the gun and pushed it away, leaped out of my chair and hollered "Oh, my God!" Security came rushing up and dragged him out the back door.

I just ask people to respect me. I have had people stop me while I was running—literally running—to catch an airplane to ask for my autograph. I have had people interrupt me while I'm eating with my family to demand—not ask, demand—my autograph. But the thing that bothers me most is people who come up to me and instead of simply saying, "How you doin', Terry? It's nice to meet you," they begin by telling me, "You know, I really used to hate you. Can you sign this to me with your best wishes?" Beg pardon? I was racing through the airport in Dallas one day, just dragging all my luggage, when a businessman stopped me and said with a big smile on his face, "I've hated you my entire life . . ."

Maybe I was just too tired to hear that again. "Then you know what?" I said. "You need to grow up and get over that, because I don't hate you. How can you say that to someone because we beat the Cowboys . . ." Once that faucet was turned on I couldn't shut it down.

He kept trying to apologize, but I wouldn't let him. "You should apologize," I continued, "your momma didn't raise you any better than to tell people you hate them? I'll bet if I called your mother right now she'd be embarrassed for you."

Another time this man waited until after I'd signed his piece of paper before telling me, "Thanks. Boy, you know I hated you when you were playing. I never have liked you—" I jerked that signature right out of his hand. I took back my autograph. I may only be me, but I do have a certain amount of pride.

I know the impact meeting a celebrity can have on people. I mean, I can remember easily the first time I saw Robert Redford in person. Robert Redford! I just wanted to look at him, size him up, see how he squared with the impression that I had of him. Same thing with Paul Newman and John Travolta. So I have people I admire too. But I had a person come up to me one time and tell me, "Terry, do you remember in 1972 you were having dinner at Tony O's restaurant in Pittsburgh and I brought my little boy over and you signed an autograph for him? I just wanted to tell you that he still has it."

Do I remember signing one autograph several decades ago? Not hardly. I can barely remember the first chapter of this book. But the fact that this man remembered it so well, that meeting me was so special to him and his son, made me feel really good.

What I don't like particularly are bad memories that some people hold tight to, memories that darken their present. We are all of us a product of our past just as surely as a sculpture was once a block of stone. What I have always tried to do in my life is minimize the damage and emphasize the positive. Whatever happened happened. It's done—unless it continues to affect your life.

In 2001 the great receiver Lynn Swann was elected to the pro football Hall of Fame, as he should have been a long time ago. But while he was being inducted he said that the reason he didn't get into the Hall of Fame sooner was because "Bradshaw did not seem like he wanted to throw the football in my direction." We lost the last game of his career, which ended with me throwing a Hail Mary into the end zone toward John Stallworth. Apparently he was so angry that I didn't throw that pass in his direction that, he admitted, "I wanted to kill him." He said that the only thing that prevented him from going after me in the locker room was seeing my dad sitting there and having too much respect for parents.

"Bradshaw's in the Hall of Fame," he continued. "He has four Super Bowl rings and is doing a terrific job at Fox. But could he read secondaries? I doubt it. Pick a guy, throw him the football. What made Bradshaw decide not to throw me more passes at the end of my career, I have no idea, no idea. I mean, socially we didn't see each other or hang out. Maybe he and John did more, I don't know."

It's real hard to have a feud with someone when the other person doesn't know about it. I was stunned when I read Lynn Swann's comments. I wondered, how long has he been carrying those feelings around with him? I had absolutely no idea he felt that way. If it had bothered him so much he could have called me, he could have written me a letter; maybe I could have cleared it up. But he didn't. We had seen each other a few years earlier and he hadn't said one word to me about being mad. So when he said those things about me, when he pointed his finger at me and made those accusations, well, truthfully I was livid. His comments made headlines in the sports pages all across the country. And I kept thinking how sad it was that he chose what should have been one of the greatest days of his life to create this controversy. Why let the past spoil such a wonderful day? Instead of using that opportunity to release some anger, he should have enjoyed all the honors due him. He should have been thrilled.

Maybe I should have responded to his charges a little more strongly than I did. When I heard about them I thought they were absolutely ridiculous, all of them, well . . . except maybe that part about me not being able to read secondaries. But I've already admitted that. I got a little better at it near the end of my career; mostly, though, I just tried to find an open receiver and throw him the football. Anybody who believes I had time or the inclination to sit back in the pocket and make a conscious decision not to throw the ball to Lynn Swann is giving me a lot more credit than I ever earned. I've spent the two decades since my retirement proving that my brain doesn't work that fast.

Maybe I didn't know Lynn Swann was mad at me because he believed I preferred to throw the football to John Stallworth because a few years earlier Stallworth had told a reporter, "I was ticked off early in my career because I felt Bradshaw was forcing the ball to (Swann) when I'd be open."

During my career I wasn't close friends with most of my teammates. Since I retired I've rarely spoken to any of them. I finally got in contact with our punter Bobby Walden a few weeks after he'd suffered a heart attack. He was cussing me out for not calling him after his heart attack. I told him, "I haven't spoken to you in twenty years and you're mad 'cause I didn't call you three weeks ago? C'mon, you shouldn't have had that heart attack till after I talked with you."

Lynn Swann and I had always gotten along. Well, at least I thought we'd always gotten along. In fact, when I was inducted into the Hall of Fame I said in my speech, "[I]n football you never get anything that you don't share with people. You don't get elected into the Hall of Fame by yourself. [So] Thank you, number eighty-eight, Lynn Swann!" That was the first name that came to my mind, the first name I mentioned. So if

I was harboring any bad feelings, they were so deep even I didn't know about them.

I didn't really know how to respond. My natural reaction was to strike back, but I caught myself and decided, I'm going to love him. I'm going to care about him. I'm going to make sure he knows he doesn't have a problem with me. If I see him on the street I'm going to hug on him. If he isn't interested in being hugged I'm still going to love him.

I did several interviews in which I was asked to respond to his remarks. I said only nice things about him. I created no harm. I just wasn't interested in allowing his past to intrude on my present. And nothing but good came out of it for me.

The day my football career ended I walked out the door and never looked back. Past is past, done is done. I was done and I knew it. To have been part of those teams, to have brought so much joy to so many people was a real blessing. But that was only the first part of my life, and I didn't want to spend the rest of it still living there. I never once missed playing the game; if I missed anything at all it was being in the locker room. That was the fun part.

For a long time after I retired, though, I did have the same dream. Now I know that a lot of you people who have been to college have the same anxiety dream; you have the last final exam that you need to pass to graduate, but you haven't attended the class all semester and don't even know where the test is being given. If I had that dream my version would be a lot more terrifying: I'd find the classroom and have to take the test. But in my football dream I'm in a game and I drop back to pass. I see a receiver wide open and I try to throw the ball but it won't . . . won't . . . come out of my hand. It's like it is sewn to my hand, I can't get rid of it. That play doesn't go anywhere, and the dream ends right there. I've never known if we won or lost that game; all I remember is a feeling of great frustration at not being able to throw the ball.

There are so many moments in my life that I just never will forget: Sleeping out on the porch at my pawpaw's house with my brothers and cousins as the summer rain pounded on the corrugated metal roof. Singing with Paul McCartney at the Super Bowl. So many wonderful moments on the football field. Walking out of the locker room after winning the Super Bowl and having my father hug me. Making a TV commercial with Alf the . . . Alf the . . . thing. Watching both my daughters being born. That time back in Shreveport my brother and I threw those water balloons at the police cruiser, or that time I shot an arrow into the air and it—well, I guess some things it's better we do forget.

We all have a collection of wonderful memories stored away. The senior prom. The first time you saw the person you fell in love with. The day you got your first real job. That time at work you didn't know the boss was listening. The day you found your new job.

I love my memories, but I try to keep churning out new ones. And while I'm doing it I also try not to worry about the future. Some people let their fear of the future affect the present. As an athlete, for example, it seems like you spend your entire career worrying about what might happen. When you begin your career there's the fear you aren't ever going to get a chance to play. Then after you win a job you become afraid of losing it. After you get established as a player you start worrying about getting injured, and as time passes you begin to worry about getting old and being replaced by a younger player who is afraid he isn't going to get a chance to play. Finally, there is the fear that after you're out of the game for a while you'll no longer be in demand and you won't be able to earn a living.

There wasn't one time in my career that I felt completely secure, that I felt like I had it made, that I could ease off the throttle and relax. Every pro football player knows he is always one play away from the end of his career. The important thing is to keep that thought out of your mind, and play like you're going to play forever.

Worrying about the future takes up a lot of time in everybody's present. Is my job secure? What happens if the company merges or sales go down or a competitor introduces a new product or the price of oil goes up or management gets a look at my E-mails? Should I buy that house, that car, those new socks, plan a vacation, fix the wringer on the washing machine, invest in stocks, loan my momma the bail money, or take those rumba lessons?

Being concerned about the future is a responsible, mature way to act. So I definitely intend to do it myself someday. Making plans for your future is smart and sensible. But living your life in preparation for your future pretty much means ignoring the present. You're going to miss a lot of life waiting for life to happen. When a sports team announces it is "building for the future" it is really admitting the present isn't going to be very good. Hey, optimism is cheap, available in great abundance and it sells. It's a lot easier to "project earnings" than actually earn them: Uh, Ted, I know right now we've just got this one dinky little candy store, but we're planning to add a high-tech digital

211

computer development center in the back room that will make our stock a great buy thank you very much. I've found that most often teams that build for the future never get there.

Before each game our coaching staff devised a game plan consisting of the offensive plays and defensive formations they thought would be most effective against that particular opponent. It was a long-range plan providing as many options as possible. That was planning for the future. But on the field we never called more than two plays ahead—and then only when we were in our "hurry-up" mode—because we never knew how successful the next play would be. We didn't know what yard line we'd be on, what down it would be, what we needed to accomplish. So we did what was necessary right at that moment. Same thing is true for life. Plan for the future but never forget what yard line you're on in the present.

One of the really difficult things about being a professional athlete is that you spend your whole childhood training for a career that ends pretty much at the beginning of your adult life. For athletes the future comes early. With the exception of those few athletes who sign contracts large enough to support them for the rest of their lives, every pro athlete is concerned about their future. One of the first things I did when I earned a little money—and with the Steelers that was generally what I earned—was buy a ranch that I could enjoy while I was playing and live on when I retired.

That was pretty much the extent of my planning for my future. Like every professional athlete I got to my future a little sooner than I might have liked, but I was very fortunate. I was able to make an entire new career out of being me.

I don't know for sure, but I believe that people watch me

because they have come to expect the unexpected. No one is quite sure what I'm going to do or when I'm going to do it. That includes the people with whom I work, the directors and producers, and me. I do try to find enjoyment every day, I do try to make life fun for the people around me, I try to live very much in the present.

Maybe the hardest question I've ever been asked is, Terry, why did you do that? I've gotten asked that one a lot. And generally it's best to reply, well, it seemed like a good idea at the time. I basically have one strict rule I follow about going through life: I don't want to hurt anybody. Other than that, pretty much anything goes. I tend to be a bit impulsive. I admit I can be silly. Like that thing with the ducks, for example. Most of you have heard the expression, as easy as shooting ducks on a pond? Well, I did better than that. One morning I woke up and looked out at my swimming pool and there were all these ducks just floating there nice and easy as if they owned it. On my pool! Whoa, no, ain't gonna happen. I thought about all those cold mornings my father and I had sat quietly freezing waiting for some ducks to show up. All those cold, cold mornings that we'd gone home without seeing one single duck. And these ducks had the audacity to light on my pool? Did they think that maybe I'd forgotten all those cold mornings? Did they think maybe there was some rule about not shooting ducks on a pool? Did they think that maybe I had grown up and got some civilization?

I don't think so. They're ducks. So I got me my shotgun and I put on my cowboy boots and marched out to the pool.

Charla was in the kitchen. I suppose she was surprised to see me walk by the window carrying my shotgun and wearing my cowboy boots, a T-shirt, and nothing else. But at that point we'd been married a long time so maybe she wasn't surprised at all. "What are you doing, Terry?" she asked.

"Ducks on the pool," I told her, "ducks on the pool." If she had asked me why I wasn't wearing any pants possibly I would have pointed out that the last time I'd been duck hunting I wore a lot of clothes and the ducks never showed up. I just didn't feel it was necessary to dress for ducks. Maybe that was an excessive use of force but I will tell you that none of those ducks have ever come near my pool again.

Mostly the things I do are spontaneous, but sometimes I do have to make a plan. Like buying those sardines for my friend Terry Rice's wedding. Maybe his mistake was asking me to be his best man. Naturally I had to do something special. So I purchased twenty-five pounds of rice, I don't know how many sardines, and the traditional shaving cream. I just drowned his car in shaving cream; so much that he drove directly from the church to the car wash before leaving on his honeymoon. But there wasn't anything a car wash could do about those sardines. I hid them everywhere in that car, under the seats, in the glove compartment, in the ash tray. Terry Rice thought he'd found them all and got 'em out of the car before he parked it in the hot sun at the airport.

Well, it turned out he didn't quite find them all; he didn't find the sardines in the engine or under the rear floor mats, for example, so they sat baking in the Texas sun while he was on his honeymoon. And we didn't quite throw the twenty-five pounds of rice—we put it in his suitcase, mixed in with his socks and shirts. Every time he went to get dressed he thought of me.

I think Terry Rice believed everything we did was funny—right up until he got back from his honeymoon and opened the door to his car. There is something about dead sardines rotting in the hot sun for a week that takes some of the humor away. I think the exact phrase Terry Rice used to describe his car was "Way past stink."

I've just always known that there are laughs hidden somewhere in every day and my job was to find them. I have a confession to make: I am to people who act too seriously what a needle is to a balloon. I get away with it, mostly, because I'm willing to make fun of myself and my family. Whatever I say about somebody else, I'm definitely going to say much worse about myself and the people closest to me. Unfortunately, I lost one of my best characters in my divorce. Any one of them. Trust me, divorce lawyers got their sense of humors from clams. Man, they just stand there with their jaws shut tight. They only open their mouths to say, "That's not funny," or "More." But after one of my divorces my own lawyer told me it would no longer be appropriate to use that particular ex-wife as a character. He said something about me not exaggerating her . . . attributes; that I shouldn't tell anybody about that one long eyebrow she's got snaking across her forehead from ear to ear and the way she kind of lifts off the ground when her ears catch the wind and . . .

It's not me saying anything like that, you understand; I'm just quoting my lawyer warning me to stop exaggerating. Of course, then I did have to tell him that I wasn't exaggerating.

Fortunately, soon after my divorce I got a brand-new character when my momma lost her other tooth. I felt so sorry for my momma, she sure had loved doing her famous beaver imi-

215

tation. And, truthfully, it was nice to have all that cut timber for the fireplace. It's true that everybody in the family just loves her to bits, but after she lost that tooth we stopped eating with her. Momma's only got that one tooth left, and it sort of hangs down when she eats. My friends, that is not a pretty sight. Nobody in the family has kissed her with their eyes open in four years now.

Tell you what I did, though; I videotaped her eating a well-done steak one night. I got her a little bitty steak and cooked it medium well. Then the family stood back and watched her working at it. The good news is that I sent the tape to the *America's Weirdest Videos* TV show and we won the $10,000. I used the money to buy her a new false tooth. Next winter's supposed to be very cold and we're gonna need the firewood.

None of that is true, of course—well, except maybe for the firewood part. But if my mother heard me tell this story she'd take a deep breath and say, Now, Terry, don't you go telling stories like that about your mother. You know that's not nice. And then after thinking about it for a minute she probably would add, Tell them about your Aunt Louise.

I can make up stories about other people because I never hesitate to laugh at myself. And the truth is it's not easy laughing at myself. Usually I want to cry. My problem is that when I look in the mirror I'm not even smart enough to know if I'm funny looking. Most of the people in life that I care about have the ability to laugh at themselves, and naturally as a good friend I'm always going to be there to help them.

For me, laughing at myself is just another way of facing reality. I'm not perfect. No, no, please don't object, it's true. I admit it. Howie Long, for example, has that chiseled look while I have more of what you might call a molded look. My old partner Cris Collinsworth has a great head of hair while I . . . while I have a head. And James Brown, my girls love JB, mostly because he can puff up his cheeks and sound like he just inhaled helium, while I sound just like a dad.

I've never known anybody who is perfect, and even if I knew you I would still be able to say that. Because you're no more perfect than I—well, you're definitely not perfect. You know that. You know there are things about yourself that you'd just love to change. I'll give you an example: You know, you have a pretty large— Okay, you go ahead and finish that sentence. I think you'll find that if you can laugh at your imperfections they won't seem so important. Years ago I learned that not treating myself very seriously made people feel comfortable around me.

One thing that does surprise me a bit is how many women come up to me at a restaurant or at the airport and tell me that their husband or boyfriend or even their dad looks just like me: No kidding, Terry, people are always mistaking him for you, you just wouldn't hardly believe it. And you know what, I swear this is true, when he tells them he's not Terry Bradshaw they don't believe him, they think he's just being humble.

That's usually the time when I tell them I'm not Terry Bradshaw either.

What often happens is they ask me to stand right where I am, Don't you move now, and go to fetch their man. They come back a few minutes later with a fat little guy about five-six, and the only thing the two of us have in common is— what? The bald head. One hundred percent of the time they are bald. I look at these people and I think to myself: You know, except for the legs, the body, the shoulders, the neck, and the head, and except for his height and weight, yeah, I can definitely see the resemblance. Can these people really think we look alike?

But most times I smile in astonishment and say something like, Wow, my momma told me I had a twin brother who got stolen away when we were born, but until right now I never would have believed it. You say your name is Jerry?

Just remember, if you're one of those people who take themselves superseriously, if you can't laugh at yourself, don't you worry about it. I promise you that there are a lot of other people already doing it for you.

Some people say that no matter what they do trouble finds them; in my life fun seems to find me. Opportunities for fun just seem to present themselves to me, although I am usually pretty quick to recognize them. I'll just be walking along in a store completely innocently and I'll discover a big sale on exploding golf balls. Exploding golf balls? My friends, if ever a product was made for me, that is it. Thank you very much, I'll take three dozen. One day my brother Gary and I were playing in a Pro-Am tournament in Portland, Maine. I was playing with Arnold Palmer and he was partnered with the great Billy Casper. Oh my goodness, was he excited. So Gary gets ready to tee off, first hole, he's nervous, playing with a golfing legend, he's ready to hit, this is his big moment.

"Uh, Gar—just a minute here," I said, "Arnold Palmer wants you to use this special ball. Let me put it on the tee for you."

Gary nestled up to that ball and he whomped at it. And that thing exploded in the biggest cloud of chalk you ever saw.

I ask you, was it really my fault that somebody happened to invent exploding golf balls and I accidentally found them?

People expect me to make them smile. Having fun is part of my job description. In ancient times I would have been known as a "court jester"; of course, the court jester was also known as "the fool." Now, that's not exactly the term I use when I fill out forms asking for a job description. But I guarantee you, no one I have ever worked with has complained about me being too serious. Well, except for those few executives at CBS who thought I should actually talk about football when I was broadcasting games. So having fun, creating fun, making people smile, is a basic part of my daily life. One of the best things about doing what I do is that generally I'm doing something a little different every day. I'm traveling somewhere, I'm speaking to a new group, I'm making a television commercial, doing my show. Pretty much every day is different, I rarely get bored, which prevents me from falling into any pattern.

In pro football defensive coaches spend hours studying films of their opponents, trying to find a pattern to their play selection. What does that team usually do on third down and short yardage? What plays do they like to run second and long? When do they have a tendency to throw the ball? If coaches can find a pattern in play selection they can shut down that offense. Conversely, our offensive coaches made sure our offense never became predictable, that we never fell into a real pattern. We might use the same formation in similar down and yardage situations, but then we would try to run something unexpected from it.

A lot of people fall into patterns in their lives. One day gets to be pretty much the same as every other day. The only difference between Tuesday and Thursday is the spelling. They do the same things with the same people the same way. Life becomes routine, predictable. Life just kind of glides by. The present is just a way to get to tomorrow, and tomorrow is no different from yesterday. Now, obviously some routine is absolutely necessary. Most people have to go to work during the week; not including us fools, of course. And we all have certain responsibilities that we have to take care of; but there are things you can do to make each day a little different from all the others. You just have to watch out for those opportunities.

In football trick plays are known as "gadget plays"; like a double reverse with a halfback option or making the tackle eligible to receive a pass. So we're talking here about the gadget plays of life.

I think this would be a fine place to admit that I hate roller coasters. I'm petrified of them. Don't like them at all. Scared to death of them. Well, let me clarify that. I don't mind the going up part at all, it's the going down part. Personally, I have never seen the fun in going as fast as possible straight downhill in an open cart: My goodness, Mary Lou, it sure felt like we were going to crash that time, wadn't that great?

No, it was not great. The problem is my daughters love roller coasters. Or at least they love watching me hating them. When we went to Knott's Berry Farm amusement park in Los Angeles, for example, the girls pleaded with me to ride the Supreme Scream. I did not want to ride the Supreme Scream. I may be a fool, but I'm not stupid. The Supreme Scream goes straight up 350 feet, then drops straight down. If you want to find out whether or not you love Jesus, you ride the Supreme

Scream. But I do love my girls madly, so to please them I agreed to go on this ride.

As you go straight up higher and higher first you look down on the top of the amusement park rides, then the peaks of nearby hills, then you look down on low-flying planes—but still you keep climbing higher, and suddenly, there it is in the distance, the New York City skyline. When you finally reach the top they just hold you there for a few seconds, they let you swing in the wind, back and forth, back and forth—Oh, man, I was sweating so badly I could see tiny little people below running for umbrellas—contemplating mortality and then they wait a little long—and drop you.

The most enjoyable part of this ride is looking back on the fact that I did it: I'm cool, I'm cool, I did the Supreme Scream, I did, yes I did thank you very much. My point is that this was a day I won't forget. People, you don't have to ride the Supreme Scream to make each day a little special. Which, personally, I find to be a very good thing. All you have to do is find a way to make the day just a little different from yesterday. Pick up the phone and call someone special you haven't spoken with in a while. Buy yourself a little present. Take a different route to work. Or even do what my brother did one day, hide in my closet and leap out to scare me half to death.

I am proud of the things I accomplished in the past and I'm not in any rush to get to the future. I like being with my girls as they grow up and I'm not looking forward to looking back on these days. I'm happy right here in the present.

I never will forget the moments before we were introduced and ran out onto the field in Super Bowl IX. That was the first biggest game of my career. I had not played well that season, I wasn't feeling all that confident. As we stood there waiting, a fan just collapsed and died of a massive heart attack right in front of me.

That certainly put the importance of a football game in perspective for me. It really is simple; live your life today as completely as possible. Don't let the fun escape. Squeeze as much enjoyment out of today as possible. Cherish today. Today, right now, make this your time. Today is a great day—if you decide it is. Appreciate the fact that today is special; I promise you there will never be another day just like it. Say it: I'm not going to worry about yesterday and I'm not going to look forward to tomorrow. I am not going to waste today.

You think Dale Earnhardt wasted one single day of his life? That man went ripping through life at 250 miles an hour. And when he got in the rut he took his hands off the wheel and he smiled. Loving every single minute of it.

Every day upright is a splendid day. Every day above ground is a gift. I don't worry about tomorrow. Tomorrow will take care of itself. I hope you don't waste your time fretting about yesterday. It's done, it's gone.

It's today. It's right now. And you're alive. And breathing. I do two things every morning when I wake up. I sit on the edge of my bed and I open my eyes and I draw in a deep breath of fresh air and I say to myself, This is good! This is very good! Thank God almighty I'm alive. I am alive!

My friends, you've got no chance if you're dead. You can't sell your products if you're dead. You can't throw a pass, hang wallpaper, hug your wife, play golf, go to church, if you're dead. So every morning, one time, each one of you, just stop, open your own eyes and say, I'm alive! Thank you, God, I'm alive. I'm gonna have me a great day. And then, after you've determined that you're alive, put a big smile on your face. I mean a big smile.

You got a lot to smile about. You are alive. If I was learning how to write in school they would definitely have me writing, over and over, I am not going to waste today. I am not going to waste today . . .

Amen to that, brothers and sisters, amen to that.

CHAPTER 12

TEAM WORKS

OF ALL THE EXPERIENCES OF MY LIFE NOTHING compares with watching my daughters—my own flesh and blood—come into this world and take their first breath, then get that well-known pop on the butt and cry out. I was standing right there, I cut their umbilical cords and set them free.

Of course, when Rachel was born first I had to put down my video camera. I learned a real important lesson that day: It's probably not a good idea to say to your wife while she's giving birth, "Smile, dear." I remember I was playing with Rachel's hair as she was being born, twirling it in my fingers. There was something magical about my baby being born with more hair on her head than I had. Erin arrived too quickly for me to get it on tape; she couldn't wait to get here.

I had been there for the birth of a lot of cattle, a lot of horses, but watching my own child being born made me just want to get down on my knees with appreciation and gratitude. The first time I held my own babies—it was a thrill beyond anything I had ever thought possible. Think of it as human superglue; the strongest bond possible.

My pawpaw, my grandfather, died in his sleep in a hospital.

I loved that man. He was a poor man by financial standards but a rich man in his heart. He had a small piece of land, raised some cotton, and had a few head of bony cattle. He appreciated life; he loved people, loved to hunt and fish and basically raised all the food he ate. He fashioned the harnesses for his two Clydesdales out of cypress. When I was young he would sit back in his recliner in front of a little old stove and I would brush his hair. Many years later, when he was old, I'd send him a carton of Red Man chewing tobacco every week and he would just brag about that to his many friends.

Life and death, it doesn't get any simpler than that. We come into this world with the love and the help of other people and if we're very fortunate we leave it with the love of a lifetime. What makes it all matter are the people whose lives we touch, the people we love and who love us—our family, our friends, the people we meet with and work with every day, and even those people whose paths we cross only once. The impact we make on this world isn't defined by a star in a Hollywood sidewalk or a bust in the football Hall of Fame or the amount of money we make, it is how we affect the lives of other people.

We're all in this together. One way or another we're all dependent on each other. I could have been the greatest passer in the history of the world, but no one would ever know it if I didn't have receivers like Lynn Swann and John Stallworth catching them, or an offensive line to protect me. Even the greatest salesperson in the world needs somebody to sell their product to. If you own a store, drive a cab, operate construction equipment, work in the financial business, whatever you do, you are dependent on other people. What good is a dentist without the teeth of others?

Whether you're talking about your own family, your company, a team, a club or group, you are going to be dependent on other people for success. There was a good reason there never was a comedy act called The One Stooge. You all have got to work together for the common good. If you don't believe me, just close your eyes and imagine what would happen if every player in a marching band decided to march in their own direction!

The very best feeling I ever had as a football player was to walk out of the locker room after a game and see my family waiting there for me. From high school through all four Super Bowls—win or lose—they were always there for me. My mom, my dad, my Uncle Duck. My brothers. I can't even imagine how lonely it would have felt to have achieved success, I mean any kind of success from winning the Super Bowl to being the leading salesman, or having the number-one-rated TV show, or putting out the number-4,516-ranked CD, and not have people you love to share it with. What good are all of the honors you receive if you can't say to your family and friends, thank you, we did this together, thank you. I mean, people, how much fun is it to be the only person at a celebration barbecue?

Conversely, it would have been really tough for me to get through some tough times in my life without the support of my family and friends. My situation in Pittsburgh became so unpleasant one year early in my career that my mother moved up there and stayed with me for several months to help me get through it. It didn't matter to her how badly I played; after every game she'd look at me with love in her eyes and try to cheer me up. "No matter how awful you were out there," she'd tell me, "and even though you threw four interceptions, that's four, and even though you had a receiver so wide open in the end zone that I could have completed the pass, and even though you fumbled twice, and even though you called plays against the zone when they were playing man to man, even with all that, I still like you."

Actually she was a lot more supportive than that. She was there for me when I pretty much didn't leave my apartment because I was afraid I'd be booed by my very own doorman. Things were really tough for a while in Pittsburgh. How tough was it? I'll tell you how tough it was: I was the only person in the city to whom the Department of Sanitation made deliveries! Ba-dum-dum. That's how tough it was. But my momma was there. She took care of me when I needed it most. We stayed together, we played a lot of cards to pass the time and it worked out great. I won about four hundred bucks.

My family was a team, all working together toward the goal of the best possible life for all of us, and my teams have been families. Most teams never grow together; they're just basically a group of people sharing a locker room for a time, but the Pittsburgh Steelers grew up together into champions. At some point in our careers every one of us has been the new guy, the person who doesn't know where the rest room is. Well, we find out pretty quick; or if we don't find out we embarrass the heck out of ourselves and forget all about going to that job again. You walk into an office or a locker room as an individual, but in the best situations you become part of the group and the group becomes a family.

Listen to this: Many, many people spend more waking hours with their co-workers than they do with their own flesh and blood. If you don't learn how to care for each other there is no possible way you will grow as a group, as a company. Every team we played against had exactly the same number of players we did—but not one of those other teams kept most of their players together as long as we did. And not one of those teams got as many players as we did at the very beginning of their careers through the draft or free-agent signings. We grew together, we knew each other's families, we cared about each other; we won together and we lost together. You certainly are an individual, you're the only you, but you are better and stronger and more productive as part of a team.

You know how I ended up with the Steelers? Because they were the worst team in professional football. Actually they were tied with the Chicago Bears as the worst team in pro football. Each team had won only one game; but the Bears' victory was over the Steelers. The Steelers were so bad they got first pick in the annual draft and I was their first selection. How did it feel to be picked by the worst team in pro football? A team that had won only one game? Great. It was fabulous. The worst team in pro football was still in pro football. And to me the Steelers weren't a bad team; it was my team and I was certain I could help make my team a winner. My first season we won five games and lost nine. But there was never one day that I thought of us as losers; far as I was concerned we were winners in training. It was just a matter of when.

Probably because the core of the team played together so long we thought of ourselves as a family. Almost every member of the team grew up in the family. Between 1969 and 1980 the Steelers only acquired five veteran players—people who were playing on other teams—in trades. That makes sense to me. If your family needed a new brother would you trade with another family for an established brother then try to make him fit into your family, or would you get a baby and raise him to be your brother?

Every single member of that team contributed to our success. Players, coaches, trainers, mothers-in-law . . . We had the smallest offensive line in the NFL. One year our offensive line coach Dan Radakovich thought we were getting tossed around too much by bigger defensive lineman. Those big people would just grab tight to Moon Mullins or Jim Clack's jersey and kind of toss them out of the way. So our equipment manager Tony Parisi got his mother-in-law to tailor our linemen's jerseys. Tailor? She made them so tight the defenders couldn't grab hold of them. Then to make it even harder we sprayed the jerseys with silicone and taped them to the shoulder pads with two-sided tape. For the defensive linemen it was like trying to get a grip on marble.

We had a lot of individual stars on that team, and every single one of them had a big ego. Any player in pro football who claims he doesn't have an ego is lying. After almost every play I had people coming back to the huddle all excited telling me, "Throw me the ball, T, you gotta throw me the ball this time. I got my man set up."

And then I'd have to put a compassionate hand on his shoulder and tell him, "Nice going, son, but you're a guard, you're not allowed to catch the ball."

I remember hearing coaches tell the team, "There is no 'I' in team." Actually, we debated that for about an hour—we were football players not English majors—and we looked it up in the dictionary and found out it was true. Of course, we later found out that there is no pig skin in a "pigskin." And in those early years at least, there was no money in our contracts.

The Steelers were so good for so long because we were all able to put away our egos for the good of the team. The pride we took in playing a role on one of the greatest teams in football history was much greater than the satisfaction we would have gotten from greater individual accomplishments. Hey, do you ever hear me brag about the fact that I threw more than two hundred interceptions in my career? No sir, you never do, not one word.

On other teams I might have had the opportunity to throw the football more than I did. And I would have loved it, because I loved throwing that football. Just loved it. But our offense did not focus on passing; we were a power team. Did I mention how much I loved passing the football? But what the team needed me to do was give it to Franco Harris or Rocky Bleier and don't get in their way. Statistically a quarterback is sort of like a baseball pitcher; he gets credit for winning games. Terry Bradshaw won four Super Bowls. Trust me, people, I didn't win one Super Bowl. The Steelers won four Super Bowls, and I played my role on those teams. Me claiming credit for those victories would be like the rooster claiming credit for the morning eggs: Oh yeah, oh yeah, did it myself, all by myself. Hen? What hen?

If I really was so terrific, what happened to all my talent when my teammates got older or injured and began retiring? How come I couldn't win the Super Bowl by myself? The reality is that we were all in it together, I knew that; just like you and your family know it and you and the people you work with know it. We were a team. Look, it really is pretty simple; the better you perform the more success your team—your company, your family, your class, your marching band—is going to have; the more success your team has, the better your life is going to be. The Steelers had such tremendous success that just about every one of the players got individual acclaim. In the late 1970's twenty-one players made national television commercials. As a team we created a brand name, we were the Pittsburgh Steelers. We were champions.

I'll tell you something else; not everybody on the Steelers loved every single one of their teammates. At times it was not exactly a love-in. We didn't all wear the same bowling shirts or vote for the same political candidates or, although this is hard to believe, some people didn't even like good country music. Truth be told, we had some people on that team who did not like each other at all. But for the good of the team we learned how to get along with one another. Not only that, we learned how to work together.

Don't expect to like every person you work with in an office or in a group; even in families there are people who just aren't going to like each other very much. I know that to be true because I read "Dear Abby," and if everybody got along she'd be pumping gas in Encino. And, my friends, I'm sorry to have to tell you this, as nice and kind as you are, there are some people who are just not going to like you. Whatever you do, they're not going to like you. When that happens you have to accept the fact that all human beings are different and have different likes and dislikes, and you have to be mature about it and simply understand that anybody who doesn't like you is completely out of their mind and not to be taken seriously. How could anybody not like you? Not like you? What is wrong with them?

Look, you can't please everybody. The fact is that it wouldn't have made any difference at all if I had liked Lynn Swann more than John Stallworth, or Stallworth more than Swann, or if I didn't like either one of them, or liked one of them more sometimes but not other times. My responsibility was to get the football to the open receiver. If one of our offensive linemen didn't like me—now don't get upset, this is just hypothetical—he still would have protected me because his job was to keep me alive. Each of us did our job to the very best of our ability for the good of the team—and for the paycheck at the end of the week. We worked as a team, but we got paid as individuals. Win or lose we were going to get paid, but we were going to get paid more if we won. So even if you don't particularly like someone you work with, you still throw them the pass when they get open—for your own sake.

I did get along fine with my teammates, although I didn't have any real close friends on the team. We had a lot of really good people on the Steelers, people I just respected the heck out of, but I just didn't hang out with my teammates. When we weren't at the stadium I was pretty much a loner. That was me, just being Terry. I'm one of those people that when you're with me I will focus on you and only you, I will give you my full attention and I'll mean it and, tingle or not, we will have a good time. But when we're not together I might not focus on you so much. Instead my mind will be focusing on whatever it is I'm doing at that moment, whether it's making a TV commercial or cutting hay. Recently, one of my costars in a 10-10-220 commercial complained about exactly that to me, telling me that he resented the fact that when we were working together I acted like he was a good friend, but as soon as the cameras got turned off I forgot all about him. I never called, we never had dinner together.

I had to explain the harsh facts of life to him. "Alf," I said, "you're a puppet. You're made out of cloth. When you're not making commercials or TV shows they fold you up and put you away in a box. You don't eat. You don't even have a telephone. Instead of going to the doctor you go to the furrier." I didn't want to hurt his feelings, but I was truthful.

We all want to be loved and appreciated. Even Alf. That's the basic human and puppet need. We all want other people to tell us how wonderful we are. But generally it doesn't work that way. In my career it wasn't just a few people who didn't like me, I was disliked by whole cities. Anybody asked me if I had any enemies I would have had to answer honestly, Dallas, Texas. Maybe Oakland, California. It was part of the game and it didn't bother me. Being booed in other cities was sort of a compliment: We don't like you because you're good. Play badly, we'll love you. The worst you do the more your competition is going to like you: Ah, we love old Terry, that boy ain't completed a pass since the flood of aught-four.

There are always going to be people who are going to resent your success, people who will do everything they can to bring you down. You have to understand that and not allow it to affect you. Don't pay attention to them; I'm warning you, do not listen to them. Believe me, if I had listened to critics early in my broadcasting career I'd be out there pumping gas with Dear Abby: Hey, Ab, I got that last Buick, you get this one. And don't forget to check the oil.

I kept working at it, I got better at it, and eventually I succeeded. And I am proud to say that I did it all by myself—well, except for Verne and Greg and JB and Howie and Cris and the hundreds of people at CBS and Fox whose job it was to produce the broadcasts and help me overcome all my little difficulties. Believe me, I know how much I owe to all those people—there is no possible way I could have succeeded without all of their efforts—all of them with the exception of that executive who wrote me a memo asking me not to talk so Southern and suggesting I not sweat so much.

Fox NFL Sunday is to pregame football shows what the Steelers were to the NFL in the 1970's. I think that viewers like the show because it's so obvious that we enjoy doing it. For the last few years there were four of us at the desk; James Brown, Howie Long, Cris Collinsworth and me. Like Jimmy Johnson and Ronnie Lott before him, Cris has departed, leaving the three of us who have been there from the beginning. Each of us has had a well-defined role on the show. JB is our very intelligent moderator who doles out time to each of us. Howie is our very intelligent chick magnet who combines a great knowledge of football with the potential of brute force. And I'm the very . . . the very . . . Okay, I'm the class clown. My job is to make people laugh by provoking Howie while not getting caught by JB.

What's obvious to viewers is that we really like each other. That's something you can't fake. Nobody created roles for us to play. We're just ourselves, and we pretty much play the same roles no matter what we're doing. If we were a space shuttle crew flying to the moon, for example, James Brown would be our pilot. We trust him, we depend on him. He would understand all the instruments and keep the ship flying. He'd also be busy keeping the rest of the crew under con-

235

trol, scolding us, "Would you guys please be quiet so I can see what planets we're going by? You don't want us to be shooting off into another dimension, do you?" Howie Long would be our copilot and navigator because Howie is extremely intelligent and very good at details. On the ground he'd be head of security in case a battle broke out. If Cris went with us he would be the engineer; he'd be monitoring all the computers while looking over JB's and Howie's shoulders asking endless questions like, "Are you sure that's the right moon?" My job would be food and beverage service during the trip. I would also be in charge of conducting all the weightless experiments involving peanut butter, as well as communicating with NASA to make sure they didn't forget about us. When we landed on the moon my job would be to hop out and try to make friends with the natives, maybe teach them how to play golf; I'd probably be the one responsible for changing the oil too—but the whole time we were there I'd secretly be nervous that the rest of the crew was going to close the door and take off without me hoping for a restful trip home.

Each one of us was successful before we got together, but we are far more successful as a group than any one of us was individually. The whole is greater than the parts, which is probably the best possible definition of a team. Or a family.

And it isn't just us, or the segments featuring the beautiful Jillian Barberie and the . . . the . . . less beautiful Jimmy Kimmel—I need to be charitable here, folks—we've got a large supporting crew sitting behind the camera working toward a single, unified goal: Please don't let Terry embarrass us all this week. These people are all valuable members of the team. I'm going to admit something right here: I have more people helping me get ready to do the show than Alf does. I've got producers and associate producers, directors, lighting people, makeup people—fortunately I'm allotted double time with the makeup person because Howie is so naturally perfect he doesn't need any makeup—and camera people, publicity people, and the information people who make us look smart.

In our production meetings we'll have as many as fourteen people planning the show. At that weekly meeting we'll work out every detail, we'll choreograph our movements, we'll decide what subjects we're going to discuss and lay out a rough order in which we'll speak. And once we've got that down we'll just pretty much forget about everything we've planned and go do the show.

Basically, the production meeting is our way of getting the planned show out of our system, allowing us to get down to the usual organized chaos. In the production meeting we'll all be entirely honest about a subject, maybe I'll relate a story told to me off the record about a player not getting along with his coach, for example, and I'll say exactly what I feel about it. At times I'll be pretty critical. And then someone will ask me, are you really going to say that on the show? And I'll stand up proud and strong and say, are you kidding me? No possible way.

I have a pretty good idea what points I'd like to make during the show, but I don't have the slightest idea what JB or Howie intend to say—or how I'll respond. That's one of the things that makes the show so exciting to do. During the week we each gather most of our own inside information using numerous sources we have carefully nurtured and developed over a long time; either that or we'll just make it up. And if anybody questions the source of our information we blame it on John Czarnecki.

Every team, every office needs a John Czarnecki. A good solid responsible person you can blame for everything that goes wrong. If our information seems questionable, blame John Czarnecki. The food's cold, blame John Czarnecki. I do.

Officially John Czarnecki is our league source. He probably knows more about what's really going on inside the National Football League on a week-to-week basis than anyone else in America. It's his job to dig up news or verify the information we've uncovered. When he gets a particularly good piece of information he'll give it to one of us to use on the show. Naturally I never complain that he gives his very best information to Howie or JB because I'm a team player and it really doesn't bother me that he always gives his best stuff to Howie or JB because I know that the better we do individually the stronger the show is, so it actually benefits me that he gives his most exciting information week after week after week to Howie or JB leaving me out there all by my lonesome with just the meager little tidbits I've been able to find myself. No, I don't complain at all.

I don't complain because John Czarnecki is part of the team, part of my Fox family. He's sort of like my ex-brother-in-law who opened a fish farm then went out of business when he tried to brand his fish. We don't talk about him too much, we just blame him.

I may not like getting on an airplane every weekend to fly to California to do the show, but once I'm there I can't wait to get to the studio and see everybody and get started. I love the people I work with. I love my bosses, my producer, and my director. I love the camera people, I love the set. I love our sponsors. I love putting on those elaborate costumes. I have a passion for that show. Everybody understands everybody else; each week is almost like a huge family reunion. Except there's no Aunt Louise who is constantly pinching everybody's cheek and telling them how much they've grown.

Can you just imagine how depressing it would be to have to get on that airplane and fly to California and spend that time with people whose company I didn't enjoy, doing a show I didn't like? What it might be like, for example, if Fox traded me to another network.

I do know how fortunate I am to be able to do work I love with people I enjoy. Even Kimmel. I know how lucky I am to have been able to establish myself in broadcasting after a successful playing career. While receiving the star on Hollywood Boulevard and an Emmy Award for my work were gratifying— although when other people on the show, not to mention any names, Howie, won their Emmy Award I did call to congratulate him on winning his Enema Award—being honored with the first award for sports broadcasting given by *TV Guide* was a thrill. Generally I'm not a person who cares much about awards; you won't find many of them of any kind in my house. Awards generally are subjective; you win one year and the next year against much the same competition you don't win: Gee, Terry, how'd you get so bad in only one year? Remember last year, when you were so good? What happened to you?

This one mattered to me because I was the choice of 1.5 million viewers. To me it meant that almost two decades of patience, perseverance, and hard work had really paid off for me. It wasn't going to affect my career; my future in broadcasting is determined by the people I work for, not by awards, but it really felt nice to receive it. I had finally achieved success in this field.

That's really what we all want in our careers, isn't it? Approval. People to tell you that you're doing a good job. Statistics never tell the whole story: If a quarterback completes a high percentage of his passes while his team gets beat has he been successful? If JB or Howie or Cris or I win an Emmy but the show gets beat in the ratings are we successful? If the chicken crosses the road to get to the other side but has been trying to do it for so long it forgets why it wanted to cross the road in the first place is that chicken successful?

But when your customer, your consumer, your client, whatever you call the people you are doing your job to satisfy, let you know that they appreciate your work, that is the definition of success. It's also the definition of "new contract."

Being a broadcaster, a speaker, a commercial spokesperson is my job, it's what I do, but it's not who I am. I don't want to be identified by my work any more than you do. In ancient times people were named after their work; a barrel maker was named Cooper, a tailor was Taylor or Weaver, a gardener was Gardener, a divorce lawyer was Shyster or Crook. But we don't do that anymore. Otherwise my name probably would be Talker or Singer, or just Fool. And if my jobs disappeared I would just find other things to do. What matters to me in my life are other people; my family, my children, my friends and the people whose path I cross.

CHAPTER 13

KEEP IT SIMPLE

ONE INSTANT AFTER YOU PUT DOWN THIS BOOK YOUR LIFE MAY change forever. You may walk outside and trip over somebody, you may knock off their glasses, you may get in your car and back into another car—and who knows what the result of those encounters might be? We just flat don't know. Can't even guess. We don't know from one moment to the next when our lives are going to interact with someone else and make a difference in both lives. Now truthfully I don't know you personally, I don't know anything about you—although I'm sure we'd be friends— but I do know one thing about you: You are in charge of your life. You are in control. You make the decisions. If you want to be happy, smile, be happy. You want to be a difference maker in someone else's life or in the world? Then just go ahead and do it.

I know you can't do the big things: World peace. Eternal happiness. Daily bliss. You can't change the world, but you can affect one little piece of it. Touchdowns are usually the end result of a dozen or more plays; sometimes the biggest play on a drive was less than ten yards. But we kept grinding it out, play after play, until it made a difference. Small things can make a big difference. If you don't think so remember back to when you got that brand new car, that beautiful new car that you'd dreamed about owning? Oh, my goodness that car was so beautiful. And that aroma? That new-car smell? It was perfect, just perfect. It made you so proud. You were so happy you floated through the day, you just couldn't wait to get back behind the wheel of that shiny new car. Everything in your life seemed possible.

And then the worst possible thing happened: You got a tiny little scratch on the door. It was only a little scratch, it was barely visible. Nobody else would ever notice it. But you noticed it. You saw it. It was a scratch. And you couldn't stop thinking about it. That car wasn't perfect anymore. The world didn't seem quite as bright. That one little scratch made all the difference.

Little things matter. You think it's hard to make someone feel good? It's not, just drive your car into an auto repair shop and tell the mechanic there's a loud knocking coming from underneath the hood and you don't know anything about cars, and watch his face light up with joy. Tell a woman she's beautiful. Tell a bald man you always thought hair was overrated. It's easy to make another person happy.

I promise you something right here: You lift somebody else up it's going to come right back to you. Have you ever heard one person in an audience laugh? Not likely, laughter is infectious, laughter makes other people laugh. When I'm talking to a large group and I say something funny—it happens—and they start laughing, do I feel bad? Oh jeez, they're laughing at me again. No I don't, I feel great. And I can't help smiling. By making other people happy I'm making myself happy, what could be better than that?

These are all simple things. There is nothing complicated

about it at all. Sometimes I think we're getting too smart for our own selves. We complicate life beyond necessity. We overlook the basics, the simple things. I know that life is not always easy. Believe me, I know that. It isn't exactly as we want it to be. Sometimes there just is no tingle. You can choose to spend your time focusing on negative things or understand they are part of life and move on.

Is my life perfect right now? Of course it isn't. If I could change some things I would do it in an instant. Did that young woman I dated think she was special because there was no tingle? Well, let me tell you, she wasn't. I've been with a lot of women who haven't tingled. I'm alone right now. I'm a single man. I'm definitely available. That's not what I want in my life. It makes me sad. I've got this wonderful life and no one to share it with me. A partner would make my life much more enjoyable.

But it isn't easy for me to find someone. I need to find someone that my girls approve of and they're just brutal about most of the people they meet: She's interesting, Dad, I never quite saw anyone with feet like that. My daughters always think the women I date are too young. After one date, for example, Erin asked me, Did you have a nice time at the prom? Rachel told me she approved of one woman she met because it was about time I dated somebody out of high school.

There are times I get very lonely. I see other people involved in good healthy relationships and I wonder why I'm alone. I know what I want now; I want someone with whom I share my faith and my interests, someone I find attractive, and someone who understands when they marry me they're really marrying the whole extended Bradshaw family. And that means friends as well as relatives. My family tells me I need to meet someone who loves horses, loves my family, loves me, and loves the Lord. I know they're right. But I worry that I may never find that person.

So I'm not happy about being single. And I'm not real happy about my horse business. I've invested a lot of money in my horses and haven't had much financial success. The difficulty is that I love horses. I grew up riding horses with my family. It's always been hard for me to separate my passions from my wallet. I am getting better at it though. We used to name all my horses. I had a beautiful filly, so beautiful that when I looked at her I saw the face of an angel. So we named her Face of an Angel. When I was going through my divorce there were a lot of stories in the tabloid press, so I named a colt The Tabloid Kid. I had another horse I named after Peter Sellers's bumbling detective, Inspector Clouseau—that turned out to be accurate; the horse ran into a fence and died. Maybe I didn't give them the right names. For example, maybe I should have named one of them All My Money. That way when it ran past me I could say, there goes All My Money.

But once you name a horse you make an emotional attachment. It made it too difficult for me to sell them. So I don't name my horses anymore. Doing as much traveling as I'm forced to do doesn't make me happy; it makes me feel like my roots aren't planted deep enough.

Being a divorced father makes me really unhappy. I don't see my girls nearly as much as I'd like to. I take them with me on trips whenever possible, and I try to convince them never, ever to go out with boys but I think I'm losing that battle. It hurts my heart every time I have to drop them off at their mother's house.

So my life is a long distance from perfect. I try hard not to repeat the mistakes that I've made, but that's hard for me. I can't change my nature. But at least I've begun to recognize the symptoms. I know where I'm strong and where I'm weak and I know when I'm at a crossroads. Unfortunately, I don't always take the right road. Sometimes I opt for the temporary fix rather than the long, steady path.

I get through the days by focusing on the positive things in my life, by trying to enjoy each moment and bringing as much pleasure to other people as I can. I have definitely made some progress in my life: Growing up I was always worried that people were laughing at me, and now it bothers me when they don't.

One time somebody suggested I title my speech, "Everything I Know I Learned in the Huddle." Well, I did learn some important lessons in the huddle: Don't spit when you're wearing a faceguard. Don't hug big guys who sweat too much and then try to pass a football. Don't high-five an excited 310-pound lineman and expect to regain the feeling in your hand that day. And nobody is ever going to be carrying change for a $20 bill.

The things I really learned in the huddle aren't going to make any difference in your life—unless you end up quarterbacking for Chuck Noll. I think by now I've proved that I can't give you good advice about investing your money, assuming you want to keep some of it. And I think by now I've proved that I can't give you good advice about finding and winning the person of your dreams. And I definitely believe I've proved that I don't know how to succeed in business. But what I do know are the simple things that make life better.

Keep it simple. Smile a lot. Be nice to other people. Get on the telephone and call those people who matter, wherever they are, and tell them you love them. My parents are just thrilled when the phone rings and they hear me say, "Dad, I just called to tell you I love you, man. It's Terry. Terry Bradshaw." Take time to play with your kids, write a letter or send an E-mail to someone. Pause to praise the Lord and if you don't believe in the Lord just look at the world around you and take a deep breath and be happy you're alive. Take that real deep breath right now. There, I've proved it. You are alive, Glory Hallelujah, you are alive. These are all simple things, none of them require preparation, they don't require batteries or assembly, you can't buy them at the Wal-Mart. They don't even require a PE degree. Be courageous, don't be afraid to take a chance and fail. Don't be afraid to smile wide and talk to a stranger. Don't undermine yourself. Don't hesitate to do silly things; go ahead and get on the roller coaster. I am talking about the simple things that make a person happy.

When I was playing in Pittsburgh I raised homing pigeons and raced them. The only thing that mattered to these pigeons was getting home. No matter how far away I took them, they would do whatever was necessary to get home. And they could not be fooled, they couldn't be retrained to go someplace else; they lived to come home. Obviously we are a lot more complicated than that, but isn't that what we all want out of life, a place to come home to?

Keep it simple. Sometimes you just have to get back to the basics. Have fun in your life. Life is too short to spend it getting stressed out. Find some strength and some faith. We are all searching for the same thing, a hand to hold and a heart to understand.

Thank you for coming to my book.

Life is a joy.